BEST

NONFICTION

Introductory Level

7 Selections for Young People

with Lessons for Teaching the Basic Elements of Nonfiction

Christine Lund Orciuch

Theodore Knight, Ph. D.

JAMESTOWN PUBLISHERS

a division of NTC/Contemporary Publishing Group
Lincolnwood, Illinois USA

Cover Design: Steve Straus
Cover Illustration: Michael Steirnagle
Interior Design: Steve Straus
Interior Illustrations:
Unit 1: James Porto/FPG International LLC.; Unit 2: © Adam Jones/Photo
Researchers, Inc. (page 26); Unit 3: © NTC/Contemporary Publishing Group, Inc.
(page 58); Unit 4: © National Aeronautics and Space Administration (NASA) (page
84); Unit 5: © A'Lelia Bundles, the Walker Family Collection, Alexandria, Va.
(page 120); Unit 6: © Habans-Sygma (page 150);
Unit 7: © L. Rebmann/Explorer (page 190)

ISBN: 0-89061-898-4 (hardbound)
ISBN: 0-89061-882-8 (softbound)

Published by Jamestown Publishers,
a division of NTC/Contemporary Publishing Group, Inc.
4255 West Touhy Avenue,
Lincolnwood (Chicago), Illinois 60712-1975, U.S.A.
© 1998 NTC/Contemporary Publishing Group, Inc.

4 5 6 7 8 9 10 11 12 13 14 044/055 09 08 07 06 05 04 03 02 01

ACKNOWLEDGMENTS

Acknowledgment is gratefully made to the following publishers, authors, and agents for permission to reprint these works. Every effort has been made to determine copyright owners. In the case of any omissions, the Publisher will be pleased to make suitable acknowledgments in future editions.

"Where Is Cyberspace?" by Claire Benedikt. From *Odyssey*'s November 1994 Issue: *Cyberspace*, © 1994, Cobblestone Publishing Company, 30 Grove Street, Suite C, Peterborough, N.H. 03458. Reprinted by permission of the publisher.

"Another April" from *Tales from the Plum Grove Hills* by Jesse Stuart. Copyright © 1942, 1946 Jesse Stuart. © Renewed by Jesse Stuart and Jesse Stuart Foundation. Used by permission of the Jesse Stuart Foundation, P. O. Box 391, Ashland, Ky. 41114.

"How to Improve Your Vocabulary" by Tony Randall. Copyright © 1985 by International Paper Company. Reprinted by permission of International Paper Company.

"Houston, We've Had a Problem" from *Apollo 13 Space Emergency* by Michael D. Cole. Copyright © 1995 by Michael D. Cole. Reprinted by permission of Enslow Publishers, Inc., 44 Fadem Road, Box 699, Springfield, N.J. 07081.

"I Got Myself a Start by Giving Myself a Start" from *Madam C. J. Walker* by A'Lelia Perry Bundles. Copyright © 1991 by Chelsea House Publishers, a division of Main Line Book Company. All rights reserved.

"A Child's Life in Sarajevo" from *Zlata's Diary* by Zlata Filipović. Translation copyright © 1994 editions Robert Laffont/Fixot. Used by permission of Viking Penguin, a division of Penguin Books USA Inc.

"River Creatures" from *The Land I Lost* by Huynh Quang Nhuong. Text copyright © 1982 by Huynh Quang Nhuong. Used by permission of Harper Collins Publishers.

CONTENTS

TO THE STUDENT

Nonfiction is literature about real people, places, and events—unlike fiction which comes mostly from a writer's imagination. When you read magazine or newspaper articles, history books, instructional manuals or guides, biographies and autobiographies, and diaries or journals, you are reading nonfiction. The life story of Martin Luther King, Jr., a science article about the latest research into heart disease, or a cookbook about desserts are other examples of nonfiction. To many people, good nonfiction is as interesting as, or even more interesting than, fiction.

Writers of nonfiction examine real people, events, and experiences in order to understand them. Like all writers, nonfiction writers try to communicate their thoughts, feelings, and ideas about a subject. They may want to explain why certain events happened, to describe an interesting person, place, or incident, or to persuade you to follow a particular course of action. An author's purpose in writing shapes his or her work.

People read nonfiction to gain understanding. They may be curious about a subject—the person, event, or idea—that the writer has chosen to write about. To keep the interest of their readers, writers must not only organize the information but also choose which facts to include and emphasize. In this book you will learn skills that will help you analyze how writers develop and organize their material to create lively, interesting works of nonfiction. By understanding how good writers communicate and by studying the works of good nonfiction writers, you can learn techniques to improve your own writing.

Each unit in this book contains a nonfiction selection and lessons that teach concepts and skills that will help you interpret the selection and understand the particular techniques the author uses to accomplish his or her purpose. Each unit also includes writing exercises that provide an opportunity to use what you learn in the lessons in your own writing.

UNIT FORMAT AND ACTIVITIES

- Each unit begins with a photograph or an illustration depicting someone or something connected with the selection. The photograph or illustration will help you make some predictions about the selection.

- The Introduction begins with background information about the selection and its author. Important literary concepts and skills are then presented, and you are given an opportunity to begin developing these concepts and skills in your own writing. Finally, there are questions for you to consider as you read. These questions will help you focus on the concepts and skills presented in the unit's lessons.

- The selection makes up the next section. It may be a complete work, such as an essay or an article, or an excerpt from a biography, autobiography, or diary.

- Following each selection are questions that test your comprehension of the events and other elements of the selection as well as your critical thinking skills. Your answers to these questions and to other exercises in the unit should be recorded in a personal literature notebook. Check your answers with your teacher.

- Your teacher may provide charts to record your progress in developing your comprehension skills: The Comprehension Skills Graph *records* your scores and the Comprehension Skills Profile *analyzes* your scores—providing you with information about the skills on which you need to focus. You can talk with your teacher about ways to work on those comprehension skills.

- The next section begins with a discussion of the literary concept that is the unit's focus. This is followed by three lessons, each of which illustrates a technique the author uses to develop that concept.

- Short-answer exercises test your understanding of the author's techniques as illustrated by short excerpts from the selection. You can check your answers to the exercises with your teacher and determine what you need to review.

- Each lesson also includes a writing exercise that guides you in creating your own original nonfiction work using the techniques you have just studied.
- Discussion guides and a final writing activity round out each unit in the book. These activities will help sharpen your reading, thinking, speaking, and writing skills.

Reading the selections in this book will enable you to recognize and appreciate the skills it takes to write interesting nonfiction. When you understand what makes good nonfiction, you become a better reader. The writing exercises and assignments will help you become a better writer by giving you practice in using the authors' techniques to make your own nonfiction writing interesting.

How to Read Nonfiction

Where is Cyberspace?

by Claire Benedikt

INTRODUCTION

BUILDING
BACKGROUND

Most schools and libraries, and many homes today, contain computers that are linked to the World Wide Web. You probably have used the Web to get information from different sources. For fun you may have called up colorful sites with moving type and musical backgrounds. Yet only a few years ago such possibilities were considered as unlikely as a science fiction plot.

When computers were invented, only scientists and mathematicians used them. They were practically unknown in private homes until the 1980s. By then universities and government agencies had invented a way to link their computers. By typing at a computer in one location, a person could gain access to and use the information stored on a computer at another location. This system of connected, or networked, computers was called the Internet, or the Net for short. Using the Net was not simple. First a computer had to be connected by phone or cable to a second computer that was part of the networked system. Then the user had to type certain codes to reach another computer on the Net. Without the right codes a

This image is an example of art created with a computer and of one artist's attempt to represent the concept of cyberspace.

1

user could not make contact. When one finally made contact and asked for something, the other computer answered in type only.

At this point in the development of the Internet, users could still be counted in the tens of thousands. Most people did not even consider using the Internet until a new computer language called hypertext markup language (HTML) was invented. HTML let computers exchange pictures across the Net and enabled users to send requests by simply clicking a mouse button. With the development of HTML, the number of Internet users suddenly mushroomed to the hundreds of thousands and then to the millions.

The informational article you are about to read was written just as the Internet acquired the power to transfer pictures. Few people outside universities and scientific institutions were familiar with the Net at that time. The average person saw no use for it. Even most Net users had not made contact with the picture, or graphical, format of the young World Wide Web. The young author of this article wanted to give people who had no experience with the Internet an idea of what was possible with this new technology.

ABOUT THE AUTHOR

Claire Benedikt's interest in computers began when she was about eight years old. The first computer she used was an Apple IIG in her school classroom. Soon she was off to a computer camp, where she learned to program. Claire's father, a professor at the University of Texas at Austin, was working on a book about cyberspace. Claire went to the university with him and began to spend hours on the school's computers. There she learned about the Internet. "Most people my age, if they were into computers at all, were deeply into BBSs (electronic bulletin board systems, where the content was limited to information the members posted). I never really got into them at all. I skipped that 'stage'—as will the kids of today—and found myself online in a global sense."

Claire enjoys reading and writing. She has published a book and many magazine articles about computers. Her first publishing experience was this article for *Odyssey* magazine. She then proposed and wrote the *Odyssey* "Online" column. For the next year or so, she explained one aspect of the Internet in every issue.

ABOUT THE LESSONS

In this unit you will read the informational article "Where Is Cyberspace?" The article will help you get a sense of the purposes, content, and organization of a piece of nonfiction. You also will consider how to evaluate and respond to nonfictional writing.

There are four main types, or *genres*, of literature—fiction, nonfiction, poetry, and drama. Poetry and drama are easily recognized because they have special formats. Fiction and nonfiction may look or sound similar. Both are examples of *prose*, the ordinary form of written and spoken language. Fiction is imaginary, or made-up. Nonfiction is about real people, places, and events. The informational article "Where Is Cyberspace?" is an example of nonfiction.

In the lessons following this selection you will learn how nonfiction differs from fiction and how to read and understand nonfiction. Lesson 1 explains how an author's purpose and audience shape his or her writing. Lesson 2 explains the various types of organization writers use to accomplish their purposes. Lesson 3 gives you various strategies for reading, responding to, and evaluating informative articles.

WRITING: PLANNING AN INFORMATIONAL ARTICLE

At the end of this unit, you will write your own informational article. The suggestions below will help you get started:

- Informational articles relate facts and ideas to readers. Someone who writes an informational article needs to know more about a particular topic than most other people do. In addition, the writer should include information in the article that many readers want or need. Your own interests may provide possible topics for your informational article. Start by making a list of topics with which you are very familiar. For example, do you know a great deal about tropical fish? Are you interested in a particular person or historical event? Do you have a doll, stamp, or coin collection? Do you have a favorite sport? List at least four topics about which you consider yourself better informed than the average person.

- If you can't come up with at least four topics that you already know about, list topics about which you'd like to learn. Have you always wondered who invented a particular item or how sunken treasure ships are recovered? What other topics would you be interested in researching?

- For each topic on your list, jot down three or four questions that your article will answer. For example, if you know much about tropical fish, you might write some of the most common questions that people ask before starting an aquarium. For example, your questions might include "What kind of water do I need to use?" "Do I have to heat the water?" and "Is it safe to put several types of fish in one tank?"

- Save your lists of topics and questions. You will use them again later in this unit.

AS YOU READ

Previewing before you read is a useful strategy that will help you understand informative articles and set a purpose for reading. Before beginning to read "Where Is Cyberspace?" preview it. Skim the title, the headings, and the photo caption. Ask yourself these questions:

- What is the article about?
- What can I learn from reading it?

As you read the article, ask yourself the following questions. They will help you recognize some of the characteristics of both the article itself and of nonfiction in general.

- Why did the author write this article? Who is the author's intended audience?
- What information does the article present and how is it organized?
- How well has the author presented the information? Has she answered any or all of the questions that you have about the topic? Has she achieved her purpose for writing the article? Why or why not?

Where is Cyberspace?

by Claire Benedikt

When you turn on your computer you **log in.** You **go** from folder to folder, or from directory to directory. You might **go in** to the **place** you keep all of your essays, or all of your games. You **open** a program, which is **in** your hard drive, or maybe **on** a floppy disk. You might have **windows** on your screen. What do the words in boldface type have in common? They're words that talk about PLACE, SPACE, and MOVEMENT. We're accustomed to using words like these all the time to describe what we do with our computers at home and at school.

The words we use are funny, though, because when we turn on our computers, we're sitting on a chair and looking at a screen. We're not *actually* going "in" anything. And when we go from folder to folder, or from directory to directory, we're not actually "going" anywhere, either. We're still sitting on a chair using a keyboard or a mouse. And even though we might organize all our school papers so that they are in one place, there's no *actual* place—just words or pictures on a flat screen. We imagine a place because it's the easiest way for us to understand what the computer is doing for us.

But imagine if you weren't sitting on a chair. Imagine a miniature version of yourself standing in a big room that you know is the inside of your computer. Along the walls are big metal filing cabinets, and the drawers are labeled

"Essays" and "Games." Music filters from behind colored doors. There's a door that leads outside, too. Now you really are logged in! You're in your computer, for real! Now when you open a folder, you actually have to walk up to the filing cabinet, pull it open, pick the folder, and take it out! It might even be thick and heavy! You know that you store all your information in your hard drive, and since this room has all your information in it, you know you must physically be standing in your hard drive!

You've just imagined a life in which all the information on your computer is physical instead of representational.[1] In this world, you are moving around using your feet instead of sitting at a desk and typing. But doesn't that sound just like life *before* computers? When everything was on paper anyway, and you had to use a pencil to write your essay? It does, and it should, because we're so familiar with the concept of information as physical, located in a space (like on paper, in a drawer), that we take those ideas with us right into our technology. The new space we've invented, the space that we move through all the time when we're on a computer *but actually sitting still*, is called "cyberspace."

Creating a Net

Computers can be plugged into each other (this is called a *network*), so you can log into computer number 1, but play the games stored on computer number 5, and computer number 30! The red door might lead to a second room, my friend's room. Her computer doesn't need to be in the same real-life room, either. Computers can be linked with different kinds of wiring like fiber optic cable[2] and telephone wire, in the walls and underground, so her computer might be on the third floor at school, while mine is in my room at home. I can go through my red door (in computer jargon this is called "logging in") and be in her computer instantly

[1] a likeness, image, or picture

[2] a bundle of fibers that are capable of sending data, information, through glass at the speed of light

despite the distance. Nearly instantaneous[3] travel over great physical space—though I haven't left my chair and have only typed a few words to make this happen—is part of the magic of cyberspace.

That magic is particularly important when we think about the door that leads outside. Outside of your house, there's probably a street with cars traveling it. The street is a link from building to building in the same way a fiber optic cable or ethernet[4] connection is a link from computer to computer. The car carries people quickly from place to place just like your communications software or computer account assists you in moving swiftly from computer to computer, no matter how far apart they are physically. If each building you see on this street has rooms in it, and each room is a computer, a whole city means 100,000 computers forming a city-wide network. Now imagine the whole world! Just as each part of the physical world is linked by sidewalks, streets, highways, and air lanes, the computers in worldwide networks are linked by thousands of bundles of fiber optic cables, ethernet connections, telephone wires, and satellite dishes. Millions of computers! This is one BIG cyberspace! It's so big that people call different parts of it different names. There's the World-Wide Web (WWW), Usenet, and the largest and most popular part that contains all of these, the Internet. You can think of the Internet as thousands of houses, libraries, universities, and companies, plus all of the sidewalks, streets, and highways between them. Because it has the most doors (instant travel!) to other places, the Internet is the largest cyberspace.

Using Words vs. Using Pictures
I've been talking about filing cabinets and doors, but only as a metaphor for what cyberspace is like. However, real

---

[3] done without delay; immediate

[4] a connection made by using airwaves

cyberspace is rapidly approaching a stage in which graphics (like a picture of a red door on your screen) are common, especially with the introduction of Graphic User Interface (GUI) information retrieval[5] software. NCSA Mosaic is one example of this kind of software that facilitates[6] Graphic Interchange Format (GIF), a kind of electronic picture viewing. It also facilitates icons and sometimes animations on the screen. But most cyberspace—especially on the Internet—is still made up of primarily text, not pictures. Words tell you where you are, what is there with you, and where you can go. There are even real-feeling cyberspace environments (called "virtual" realities since they aren't "actual") that exist completely as text. These virtual word worlds are called Multi-User Dimensions (MUDs). One primary kind of MUD is called a TinyMUD.

Some commercial companies, including America Online, CompuServe, Genie, and ImagiNation, do show you graphics (menus and icons) as well as words. Some people argue that using pictures rather than words makes the online experience more real because images are closer to what we're used to in real life. There are even projects for doing away with computer monitors altogether. Some scientists are perfecting goggles and gloves that are now being used to experience multi-sensory virtual reality. When you put the goggles on, the real room disappears and is replaced by a computer-generated room displayed by the goggles. It feels as if you're standing in a room that isn't even there! With the help of the glove, you can reach forward to pick up a book that exists only in this virtual world. One day you'll be able to put on VR goggles and see 100 people in the room with you, even though they're in other states or countries. Then cyberspace really will have arrived!

---

[5] the act of getting and bringing back; getting information from storage

[6] makes easy

REVIEWING AND INTERPRETING

Record your answers to these questions in your personal literature notebook. Follow the directions for each part.

REVIEWING

Try to complete each of these sentences without looking back at the selection.

Recalling Facts

1. The World Wide Web
   a. is part of the Internet.
   b. contains the Internet.
   c. is the same as the Internet.
   d. is totally separate from the Internet.

Understanding Main Ideas

2. Cyberspace is
   a. real space that people move through.
   b. the imaginary space people "move" through when they use their computers.
   c. the way computers are linked to each other.
   d. how long it takes a computer to send a message.

Identifying Sequence

3. According to the article, the first step in operating a computer is to
   a. open a folder.
   b. open a program.
   c. log in.
   d. go from directory to directory.

Finding Supporting Details

4. Of these links, the one that the Internet does *not* use to connect computers is
   a. telephone wires.
   b. satellite dishes.
   c. fiber optic cables.
   d. air lanes.

Getting Meaning
from Context

5. In the quotation "we're so familiar with the concept of information as physical . . . that we take those ideas with us right into our technology," the word *concept* means
a. idea.
b. law.
c. birth.
d. beginning.

INTERPRETING

To complete these sentences, you may look back at the selection if you'd like.

Making Inferences

6. From the fact that the article does not define the term *hard drive,* you can suppose that
a. the writer does not know what a hard drive is.
b. there is no easy way to define the term.
c. there is no need for readers to know what a hard drive is.
d. the writer expects her readers to be familiar with the term.

Generalizing

7. The author's attitude toward cyberspace can best be described as
a. confused.
b. excited.
c. bored.
d. disappointed.

Recognizing Fact
and Opinion

8. Of the following statements the one that expresses an opinion is
a. "The concept of cyberspace is easy to explain."
b. "Computers can be linked with different types of wiring."
c. "Some computer services show graphics as well as words."
d. "Scientists are working on ways to make cyberspace seem more real."

Identifying Cause and Effect

9. We use terms relating to space and movement to describe our interactions with computers and the Internet because
   a. when we turn on our computers, we're sitting on a chair and looking at a screen.
   b. we are familiar with using these terms to describe how we store and obtain written information.
   c. there is no other possible way to describe making use of stored information.
   d. we use space and movement when we press the keys on the keyboard or move a mouse.

Drawing Conclusions

10. From all the information provided in this article, you can conclude that
   a. computers can create real space.
   b. nobody understands the Internet.
   c. it is important for people to be aware of the Internet.
   d. computers are nothing more than metal filing cabinets.

Now check your answers with your teacher. Study the questions you answered incorrectly. What skills are they checking? Talk to your teacher about ways to work on those skills.

How to Read Nonfiction

Nonfiction is writing that tells about real people, places, and events. It includes many different forms of writing. Some forms—such as newspaper and magazine articles, historical accounts, and biographies—report and interpret actual events. Other forms—such as letters, diaries, and autobiographies—relate personal feelings and opinions. Informational articles explain how things work or how they came to be. Critical essays analyze and evaluate performances or products. These are only a few of the forms of nonfiction writing.

As you probably can guess, different forms of nonfiction call for different reading strategies. How can you choose the best strategy for reading a particular piece of writing? It is useful to start by identifying a few major characteristics of the piece. These will guide you in determining the most useful approaches to the material. They also will let you know what kind of response the writer hopes to get.

In the following lessons you will study "Where Is Cyberspace?" to find the article's most important characteristics and to see how they affect a reader's approach and response. You will focus on these issues:

1. **Purpose and Audience**   The author wrote this article for a particular reason and with a particular kind of reader in mind. When we recognize why and for whom a particular piece was written, we can better understand and appreciate the piece.

2. **Content and Organization**   Every author uses both facts and opinions, and organizes his or her information to emphasize certain ideas. To fully understand a piece of nonfiction, we need to see how its ideas are organized, which of those ideas are facts, and which are opinions.

3. **Response and Evaluation**   After we have determined the effect that the author was trying to create, we can evaluate whether he or she was successful in creating that effect.

LESSON 1 | PURPOSE AND AUDIENCE

Imagine seeing two different speakers on television one night. The first speaker is a comedian delivering a stand-up routine about the weather. The second speaker is a newscaster reporting on a violent storm that is approaching your area. Although both speakers' messages may contain similar information, their purposes are dramatically different. The first speaker's purpose is to amuse. He or she wants the audience to laugh and feel lighthearted. The second speaker's purpose is to inform the audience about the storm and to warn people about its possible effects. Unlike the comedian—whose goal is to make people laugh—the newscaster would be disturbed if people reacted by laughing.

The ways in which we listen to each speaker depend on his or her purpose. We expect the comedian to entertain and amuse us. Therefore, we listen for humorous lines, not factual information. In contrast, we expect the newscaster to provide crucial information about the storm, so we listen for specific details. At the mention of each wind-damaged home or flooded intersection, we compare the address with those of people or places we know to make sure that everyone is safe.

Knowing the speakers' purposes in the examples just described helps us choose the most useful strategies for getting the most from what we hear. In the same way, knowing an author's purpose helps us choose the most useful strategies for getting the most from what we read. Read this excerpt from "Where Is Cyberspace?" to determine the author's purpose for writing.

> . . . we're so familiar with the concept of information as physical, located in a space (like on paper, in a drawer), that we take those ideas with us right into our technology. The new space we've invented, the space that we

move through all the time when we're on a computer *but actually sitting still*, is called "cyberspace."

In this excerpt the writer defines *cyberspace*. To help readers understand this new term she stresses the similarities between physical space—a concept we already understand—and its computer counterpart. Because her purpose is to inform us of new technology by comparing it to familiar ideas, this excerpt clearly calls for us to use the reading technique of comparing and contrasting. Other excerpts may require us to use a different technique, however.

The writer's intended audience also affects the way we approach the material. Reread the preceding excerpt. From its vocabulary and sentence length, would you say the article is written for students in grade school, middle to high school, or college? Considering its explanation of the material, is the article intended for experienced computer users or new users? Your ability to read and understand the information in the article will depend upon where you place yourself in relation to the author's target audience.

EXERCISE 1

Read this excerpt from the article. Then use what you have learned in this lesson to answer the questions that follow it.

I can go through my red door (in computer jargon this is called "logging in") and be in her computer instantly despite the distance. Nearly instantaneous travel over great physical space—though I haven't left my chair and have only typed a few words to make this happen— is part of the magic of cyberspace.

1. The first excerpt in this lesson introduces the author's purpose for writing this article: to define and explain cyberspace. The excerpt in this exercise communicates the author's attitude toward cyberspace. What attitude does Benedikt want to relate to her audience? Use examples from the article to support your answer.

2. Briefly describe your own familiarity with the Internet and the World Wide Web. Then state whether your knowledge about these topics is less than, roughly equal to, or greater than the knowledge of the audience for whom Benedikt intends her article.

Now check your answers with your teacher. Review this lesson if you don't understand why an answer was incorrect.

 WRITING ON YOUR OWN 1

In this exercise you will use what you have learned so far to continue planning your informational article. Follow these steps:

- First choose one of the topics you listed in the previous writing exercise. Your topic should be one about which you already have a good deal of knowledge or about which you can easily obtain information.
- Write a few sentences that describe your audience and your purpose for writing. Do you want to address people who share your enthusiasm for your chosen topic or those who are unfamiliar with it? Do you want to inform, amuse, or entertain? What is the approximate age of your intended audience?
- Use a concept map, or web, like the one that follows, to organize your ideas about your topic. Write your topic in

the center circle. Then add the subtopics you wrote questions about in the introductory writing exercise. These subtopics should answer the most basic questions that your readers might have about your topic. Add any new subtopics that you now think belong there.

• Save your notes and your concept map for future writing exercises.

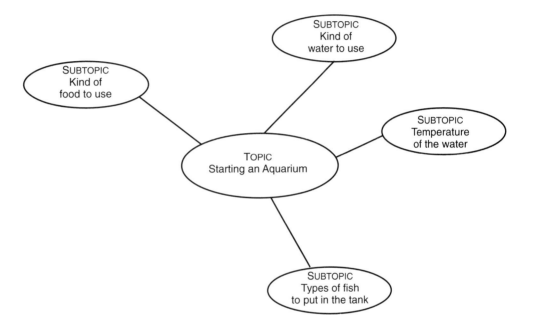

CONTENT AND ORGANIZATION

In Lesson 1 you looked at how understanding an author's purpose and identifying his or her target audience can affect your purposes for reading. Authors change their writing strategies depending upon their purposes for writing. First they select information that relates to their topic and purpose. Then they organize that information to stress particular ideas, to clarify important processes, and to share particular attitudes.

As readers we benefit in many ways from looking carefully at the content and organization of a piece. First, a careful reading of the piece helps us understand its content. When we recognize what the writer is stressing, we can see his or her purpose for writing more clearly. Then, knowing the author's purpose, we become more alert to statements that are intended to influence our thinking.

Almost all fiction is organized chronologically—that is, according to time order. This *chronological order* is also used in forms of nonfiction that relate events or describe processes—such as news stories, biographies, autobiographies, and how-to articles.

Other forms of nonfiction are organized in one or more of several different ways. Some of those ways are as follows:

Spatial order is the order of objects in a physical space. This order is used in descriptive writing. An art critic might describe a painting from right to left or top to bottom. A biologist's description of a worm might begin on the outside of the worm's body and move to the internal organs.

Order of importance is used to present facts and examples and is frequently used in persuasive writing. Information may be presented in order from least to most important, or from most to least, whichever serves the author's purpose better.

Cause-and-effect order often occurs within a piece of writing and is used to explain historic events or scientific findings.

Problem-solution order is another form of organization that makes nonfiction writing more interesting. A writer first identifies the problem and then explains proposed or actual solutions.

Often, more than one type of organization is used in a single piece of writing. For example, a historical discussion of a war may first describe events in time order. It then may list several causes and effects of the war. The causes and effects may, in turn, be ranked from most important to least important or vice versa.

Whichever organization they use, writers are almost sure to mix facts and opinions. *Facts* are statements that can be proved. *Opinions* are statements that cannot be proved and that express a person's attitudes or beliefs. Opinions also include judgments and predictions. Even when a writer does not insert an opinion directly, his or her attitude often determines which facts are used how they are arranged.

Look at the organization of the first two paragraphs of "Where Is Cyberspace?" The author begins with facts, listing terms used to describe various computer operations. Then she summarizes the information with a generalization based on those facts:

> What do the words in bold have in common? They're words that talk about PLACE, SPACE, and MOVEMENT.

Next Benedickt offers an opinion:

> The words we use are funny, though, because when we turn on our computers, we're sitting on a chair and looking at a screen.

The author supports her opinion with additional facts about what our papers and computers look like. Then she concludes with another opinion based on the evidence she has already presented:

> We imagine a place because it's the easiest way for us to understand what the computer is doing for us.

Benedikt uses a combination of facts and opinions to clarify our understanding of cyberspace as a kind of place.

EXERCISE 2

Read the following excerpt from the article. Then use what you have learned in this lesson to answer the questions.

There are even projects for doing away with computer monitors altogether. Some scientists are perfecting goggles and gloves that are now being used to experience multi-sensory virtual reality. When you put the goggles on, the real room disappears and is replaced by a computer-generated room displayed by the goggles. . . . One day you'll be able to put on VR goggles and see 100 people in the room with you, even though they're in other states or countries. Then cyberspace really will have arrived!

1. Identify at least one sentence in the excerpt that states a fact. Identify at least one sentence that states an opinion.

2. What type or types of organization does the author use in this excerpt? Explain your answer.

Now check your answers with your teacher. Review this lesson if you don't understand why an answer was incorrect.

 WRITING ON YOUR OWN 　2

In this exercise you will use what you have learned so far to add details to your informational article and improve its organization. Follow these steps:

- Review the concept map that you made for Writing on Your Own 1. Do whatever research is needed to add at least two details for each subtopic. If you were planning to write about starting an aquarium, for example, under "types of fish" you could list several species of fish that can live together in an aquarium.
- Think about the organization you will use. If you need help remembering the different types, review this lesson. Put a number next to each of your subtopics to show where each will come in your article.

- Finally, think about the details you are listing. If some details are your opinions, do you need to back them up with facts? To give yourself an idea of how evenly you are blending facts and opinions, place a check mark next to each fact, or statement that can be proved.
- Save your notes for the next writing exercise.

LESSON 3 | RESPONSE AND EVALUATION

Although you may not realize it, your response to a piece of writing often begins before you start reading and ends well after you have finished. It's usually best, however, not to make an evaluation of the piece until you have read a fair amount of it. And unless the work is so poorly written that you quickly judge it not worth your time, you should read the entire piece before making a final evaluation.

Your response to a nonfiction article such as "Where Is Cyberspace?" should begin with a preview of the piece—a fast skimming of the title, the headings, and any picture captions. This will give you a quick idea of the article's purpose, content, and organization. At this point you may be able to judge whether or not the article will be of interest to you.

As you read, you can test your predictions against what is actually in the text. For example, knowing that this article was going to be about computers and skimming the heading "Creating a Net," you might have predicted that that section of the article would be about the Internet. When you actually got into the article, however, you would have discovered that the author had something different in mind: that section of the article was actually about creating a network.

Remember to question continually as you read. Watch for connections among ideas and compare what the writer says to what you already know. Don't wait until you have finished a piece to begin questioning or disagreeing with the writer. At that point, if you realize that you missed or misunderstood something, you may have to reread the entire piece to get the answers or clarification you need.

Pause after each section—for example, before each new heading or subheading—and think about the information you have just read. Ask yourself questions such as, what have I learned so far? Do I understand what the author is saying? Do I agree with what the author is saying? At the end of the article, ask yourself these questions:

- What was the author's purpose for writing this article?
- Did the author achieve his or her purpose? If the article was meant to be entertaining, did I laugh? If it was meant to explain something, do I understand it now? If it was meant to change my thinking about something, do I think differently now?
- What, in my opinion, are the best parts of this article?
- What, if anything, could be improved?

EXERCISE 3

Skim the article "Where Is Cyberspace?" Then use what you have learned in this lesson to answer these questions:

1. State the author's purpose for writing the article. Briefly discuss whether you think she achieved her purpose. Give examples from the article to support your answer.

2. In your free time would you choose to read more articles on this topic? Give reasons for your answer. Then identify what you think are some of the strengths and weaknesses of this particular article and author.

Now check your answers with your teacher. Review this lesson if you don't understand why an answer was incorrect.

WRITING ON YOUR OWN   3

In this exercise you will use what you have learned to evaluate your plan for an informational article. Follow these steps:

- Recall your chosen topic. Decide whether the facts and ideas on your concept map are related to your intended purpose. If not, decide how to bring your notes and your purpose into balance. For example, imagine that your original purpose was to explain how to start an aquarium. Now, however, you see that most of your details are about angelfish. If you want to stay with your original topic and purpose, cross out the details that distract from the general plans for an aquarium. If necessary, start a new map. If you decide that you are actually more interested in informing people about angelfish, cross off the details that do not relate to your new topic or make a new concept map.
- Imagine yourself a member of your chosen audience. Then review your map again. Can you think of additional questions that your audience would likely have? Would additional details help? Add that information to your map.
- Think about the organization of your material. Is the type of organization you chose appropriate for your topic and purpose? Should the order be changed? Should any subtopics be rearranged? Renumber any items as needed.
- Save your work for the final writing activity.

DISCUSSION GUIDES

1. Investigate one of the people who have been influential in the development of the computer—either a pioneer such as Charles Babbage or Ada Lovelace, or a more recent developer such as Grace M. Hopper, Steve Jobs, or Bill Gates. Present a short oral report to your class about the person's life and his or her contribution to computer technology.

2. Do we rely on computers too much, or should we turn more of our work over to them? Have a class discussion or debate on this issue. Can your class come to an agreement? Why or why not?

3. The article "Where Is Cyberspace?" paints one picture of the future of computers. From your knowledge of and experience with computers, how do you expect computers to affect people's lives in the future? With a small group describe a typical day in the life of a student 20 years from now. Be specific in pointing out how the student uses computers in several situations.

WRITE AN INFORMATIONAL ARTICLE

In this unit you have learned how to plan an informational article based on what you know about a topic. Now you will use your plans to write an informational article.

Follow these steps to complete your article. If you have questions about the writing process, refer to Using the Writing Process on page 217.

- Gather the following writing assignments: 1) a list of possible topics and related questions relating to each topic, 2) a description of your audience and purpose for writing and a concept map listing details for your topic, 3) a revised concept map, a numbered list of subtopics, and notes on facts and opinions, 4) a revised plan, with reorganized material.
- After rereading what you have written so far, you will see that you have almost all the information you need for your article. Begin by writing an opening paragraph that gets the attention of your audience. This paragraph should reveal your topic and suggest your main purpose for writing, if possible.
- Next, assemble the information in your concept map. Refer to the numbers you wrote next to the subtopics. Follow this order in writing your article. If you use your subtopics as headings, underline them or write them in capital letters to make them stand out from the body of your article. Use transitional words such as *then, when,* and *therefore* to lead from one idea or event to the next.
- Finally, write your closing paragraph. You may want to repeat or summarize the main point of your article here or add a personal observation. For example, if you wrote about starting an aquarium, you could tell readers why you enjoy that hobby or why you think they will enjoy it.
- Proofread your article for spelling, grammar, punctuation, and capitalization errors. Then make a final copy and save it in your writing portfolio.

Another April

by Jesse Stuart

INTRODUCTION

BUILDING BACKGROUND

What makes a friendship special? What makes it last? As a small child, you learned the value of a friendship—it's having someone to play with, laugh with, or share something in common. Some friendships are very special. They last a long time or even a lifetime.

As people grow older, they often lose the close friendships they have relied on over the years. Many elderly people move into nursing homes or live with their children and grandchildren. They must leave friendly neighborhoods and familiar places. They must accept that they are no longer as independent as they once were and that they have to count on others to care for them. It can be a lonely, confusing time.

In "Another April" Grandpa is 91 years old. He lives with his daughter on her farm. She is very protective of Grandpa. She keeps him cooped up in the house every winter because she is afraid that he will catch a cold or slip and fall in icy weather. Come spring, however, she allows Grandpa to go outside. The selection begins with Grandpa getting bundled up for his first outing of the new spring.

People who live on farms in rural areas are especially close to nature. The seasons and the weather affect their everyday lives and work. A large barn like the one in this photo is a feature of a prosperous farm.

Under the watchful eyes of his daughter and grandson, Grandpa takes a walk around the farm. His last stop is the smokehouse, where he visits a friend— an old terrapin, a kind of turtle.

In this narrative about his grandfather Jesse Stuart describes Grandpa and his friendship with the terrapin.

ABOUT THE AUTHOR

Jesse Stuart loved the rolling green hills of eastern Kentucky. He was born in 1906 in W-Hollow in Greenup County and lived there most of his life. Stuart grew up on a farm set among the Kentucky hills. He remembered living "in a small land-locked world with no books, Victrolas (an early record player), or radios to amuse us. We didn't get a paper or a magazine and had to depend on our imaginations and what nature provided for our entertainment." Stuart's hometown, the local mountain people, and his study of nature play important roles in his many books and poems.

Besides being a gifted author and poet, Stuart was a corn and tobacco farmer and also a teacher for some 20 years. One of his books, *The Thread That Runs So True*, is about his experiences teaching in a one-room school. His other books include *Tales from the Plum Grove Hills*, from which "Another April" was chosen, and *Mongrel Mettle: The Autobiography of a Dog*. His colorful, down-to-earth stories and autobiographical works have won numerous awards. As one critic said, Stuart's stories "all have a heart."

Stuart's parents taught him to love the land and look for beauty in out-of-the-way places. From his high-school English teacher, he learned to write about what he knew best, his world in Kentucky. With this knowledge he began writing poems as a teenager. Late at night he and his old dog would hike into the hills. While his dog chased foxes, Stuart lay on the ground and wrote by lantern light.

Stuart wrote more than 40 books in his lifetime. He died in 1984 at age 77.

ABOUT THE LESSONS

"Another April" is an example of narrative nonfiction. Like writers of fiction, writers of narrative nonfiction choose language that will create the most vivid picture of the people, places, and events they write about.

The lessons that follow "Another April" focus on some ways that authors use language to tell stories about real-life experiences. Lesson 1 focuses on how the author has his or her characters speak. You will learn what dialect is and how it contributes to a story and how dialogue moves the action along. Lesson 2 explains how the choice of descriptive words—colorful adjectives and strong verbs—make a story interesting by telling precisely how people, places, or things looked, talked, or acted. Lesson 3 introduces figurative language and shows how authors use figures of speech to create strong, vivid images.

WRITING: DEVELOPING A NONFICTIONAL NARRATIVE

At the end of this unit, you will write a nonfictional narrative describing an experience that you have had. The suggestions below will help you get started:

- Think about some experiences that you will never forget. Perhaps you met someone very important or famous. Maybe you went on vacation with your family to an exciting place. Or perhaps you learned something for the first time—like how to ride a horse or bake a cake. What details about the experiences stand out in your mind? What did you learn from them?
- Make a list of at least three memorable experiences that you think would make interesting, colorful stories. Beside each, write a few brief notes describing the highlights of the experience.

AS YOU READ

Think about these questions as you read the selection. They will help you understand and appreciate Stuart's use of language in "Another April."

- What does the characters' dialect tell you about their background?
- Does the author's use of language affect the way you feel about the characters?
- What are some comparisons the author uses to make his writing more colorful and descriptive?
- Which scenes are easiest for you to picture?

Another April

by Jesse Stuart

"Now, Pap, you won't get cold," Mom said as she put a heavy wool cap over his head.

"Huh, what did ye say?" Grandpa asked, holding his big hand cupped over his ear to catch the sound.

"Wait until I get your gloves," Mom said, hollering real loud in Grandpa's ear. Mom had forgotten about his gloves until he raised his big bare hand above his ear to catch the sound of Mom's voice.

"Don't get 'em," Grandpa said, "I won't ketch cold."

Mom didn't pay any attention to what Grandpa said. She went on to get the gloves anyway. Grandpa turned toward me. He saw that I was looking at him.

"Yer Ma's a-puttin' enough clothes on me to kill a man," Grandpa said; then he laughed a coarse laugh like March wind among the pine tops at his own words. I started laughing but not at Grandpa's words. He thought I was laughing at them and we both laughed together. It pleased Grandpa to think that I had laughed with him over something funny that he had said. But I was laughing at the way he was dressed. He looked like a picture of Santa Claus. But Grandpa's cheeks were not cherry-red like Santa Claus's cheeks. They were covered with white thin beard—and above his eyes were long white eyebrows almost as white as percoon[1] petals and very much longer.

Grandpa was wearing a heavy wool suit that hung loosely about his big body but fitted him tightly round the waist where he was as big and as round as a flour barrel. His pant legs were as big 'round his pipestem legs as emptied meal sacks. And his big shoes, with his heavy wool socks dropping down over their tops, looked like sled runners. Grandpa wore a heavy wool shirt and over his wool shirt he wore a heavy wool sweater and then his coat over the top of all this. Over his coat he wore a heavy overcoat and about his neck he wore a wool scarf.

The way Mom had dressed Grandpa you'd think there was a heavy snow on the ground but there wasn't. April was here instead, and the sun was shining on the green hills where the wild plums and the wild crab apples were in bloom enough to make you think there were big snowdrifts sprinkled over the green hills. When I looked at Grandpa and then looked out at the window at the sunshine and the green grass, I laughed more. Grandpa laughed with me.

"I'm a-goin' to see my old friend," Grandpa said just as Mom came down the stairs with his gloves.

"Who is he, Grandpa?" I asked, but Grandpa just looked at my mouth working. He didn't know what I was saying. And he hated to ask me the second time.

Mom put the big wool gloves on Grandpa's hands. He stood there just like I had to do years ago, and let Mom put his gloves on. If Mom didn't get his fingers back in the glove-fingers exactly right, Grandpa quarreled at Mom. And when Mom fixed his fingers exactly right in his gloves the way he wanted them, Grandpa was pleased.

"I'll be a-goin' to see 'im," Grandpa said to Mom. "I know he'll still be there."

Mom opened our front door for Grandpa and he stepped

---

[1] mountain dialect for *pecan*

out slowly, supporting himself with his big cane in one hand. With the other hand he held to the door facing. Mom let him out of the house just like she used to let me out in the spring. And when Grandpa left the house, I wanted to go with him, but Mom wouldn't let me go. I wondered if he would get away from the house—get out of Mom's sight—and pull off his shoes and go barefooted and wade the creeks like I used to do when Mom let me out. Since Mom wouldn't let me go with Grandpa, I watched him as he walked slowly down the path in front of our house. Mom stood there watching Grandpa too. I think she was afraid that he would fall. But Mom was fooled; Grandpa toddled along the path better than my baby brother could.

"He used to be a powerful man," Mom said more to herself than she did to me. "He was a timber cutter. No man could cut more timber than my father; no man in the timber woods could sink an ax deeper into a log than my father. And no man could lift the end of a bigger saw log than Pop could."

"Who is Grandpa goin' to see, Mom?" I asked.

"He's not goin' to see anybody," Mom said.

"I heard 'im say that he was goin' to see an old friend," I told her.

"Oh, he was just a-talkin'," Mom said.

I watched Grandpa stop under the pine tree in our front yard. He set his cane against the pine tree trunk, pulled off his gloves and put them in his pocket. Then Grandpa stooped over slowly, as slowly as the wind bends down a sapling,[2] and picked up a pine cone in his big soft fingers. Grandpa stood fondling the pine cone in his hand. Then, one by one, he pulled the little chips from the pine cone— tearing it to pieces like he was hunting for something in it—and after he had torn it to pieces he threw the pine-

---

[2] a young tree

cone stem on the ground. Then he pulled pine needles
from a low-hanging pine bough, and he felt of each pine
needle between his fingers. He played with them a long
time before he started down the path.

"What's Grandpa doin'?" I asked Mom.

But Mom didn't answer me.

"How long has Grandpa been with us?" I asked Mom.

"Before you's born," she said. "Pap has been with us
eleven years. He was eighty when he quit cuttin' timber
and farmin'; now he's ninety-one."

I had heard her say that when she was a girl he'd walk
out on the snow and ice barefooted and carry wood in the
house and put it on the fire. He had shoes but he wouldn't
bother to put them on. And I heard her say that he would
cut timber on the coldest days without socks on his feet but
with his feet stuck down in cold brogan shoes,[3] and he
worked stripped above the waist so his arms would have
freedom when he swung his double-bitted ax. I had heard
her tell how he'd sweat and how the sweat in his beard
would be icicles by the time he got home from work on the
cold winter days. Now Mom wouldn't let him get out of the
house, for she wanted him to live a long time.

As I watched Grandpa go down the path toward the
hog pen, he stopped to examine every little thing along his
path. Once he waved his cane at a butterfly as it zigzagged
over his head, its polka-dot wings fanning the blue April
air. Grandpa would stand when a puff of wind came along,
and hold his face against the wind and let the wind play
with his white whiskers. I thought maybe his face was hot
under his beard and he was letting the wind cool his face.
When he reached the hog pen, he called the hogs down to
the fence. They came running and grunting to Grandpa
just like they were talking to him. I knew that Grandpa
couldn't hear them trying to talk to him, but he could see

---

[3] a heavy work shoe that reaches the ankle

their mouths working and he knew they were trying to say something. He leaned his cane against the hog pen, reached over the fence, and patted the hogs' heads. Grandpa didn't miss patting one of our seven hogs.

As he toddled up the little path alongside the hog pen, he stopped under a blooming dogwood. He pulled a white blossom from a bough that swayed over the path above his head, and he leaned his big bundled body against the dogwood while he tore each petal from the blossom and examined it carefully. There wasn't anything his dim blue eyes missed. He stopped under a redbud tree before he reached the garden to break a tiny spray of redbud blossoms. He took each blossom from the spray and examined it carefully.

"Gee, it's funny to watch Grandpa," I said to Mom; then I laughed.

"Poor Pap," Mom said. "He's seen a lot of Aprils come and go. He's seen more Aprils than he will ever see again."

I don't think Grandpa missed a thing on the little circle he took before he reached the house. He played with a bumblebee that was bending a windflower blossom that grew near our corncrib beside a big bluff. But Grandpa didn't try to catch the bumblebee in his big bare hand. I wondered if he would and if the bumblebee would sting him, and if he would holler. Grandpa even pulled a butterfly cocoon from a blackberry briar that grew beside his path. I saw him try to tear it into shreds but he couldn't. There wasn't any butterfly in it, for I'd seen it before. I wondered if the butterfly with the polka-dot wings, that Grandpa waved his cane at when he first left the house, had come from this cocoon. I laughed when Grandpa couldn't tear the cocoon apart.

"I'll bet I can tear that cocoon apart for Grandpa if you'd let me go help him," I said to Mom.

"You leave your Grandpa alone," Mom said. "Let 'im enjoy April."

Then I knew that this was the first time Mom had let Grandpa out of the house all winter. I knew that Grandpa loved the sunshine and the fresh April air that blew from the redbud and dogwood blossoms. He loved the bumblebees, the hogs, the pine cones, and pine needles. Grandpa didn't miss a thing along his walk. And every day from now on until just before frost Grandpa would take this little walk. He'd stop along and look at everything as he had done summers before. But each year he didn't take as long a walk as he had taken the year before. Now this spring he didn't go down to the lower end of the hog pen as he had done last year. And when I could first remember Grandpa going on his walks, he used to go out of sight. He'd go all over the farm. And he'd come to the house and take me on his knee and tell me about all what he had seen. Now Grandpa wasn't getting out of sight. I could see him from the window along all of his walk.

Grandpa didn't come back into the house at the front door. He toddled around back of the house toward the smokehouse,[4] and I ran through the living room to the dining room so I could look out the window and watch him.

"Where's Grandpa goin?" I asked Mom.

"Now never mind," Mom said. "Leave Grandpa alone. Don't go out there and disturb him."

"I won't bother 'im, Mom," I said. "I just want to watch 'im."

"All right," Mom said.

But Mom wanted to be sure that I didn't bother him so she followed me into the dining room. Maybe she wanted to see what Grandpa was going to do. She stood by the window, and we watched Grandpa as he walked down beside our smokehouse where a tall sassafras tree's thin leaves fluttered in the blue April wind. Above the smoke-

---

[4] a building where meat or fish is preserved by drying with smoke

house and the tall sassafras was a blue April sky—so high you couldn't see the sky-roof. It was just blue space and little white clouds floated upon this blue.

When Grandpa reached the smokehouse he leaned his cane against the sassafras tree. He let himself down slowly to his knees as he looked carefully at the ground. Grandpa was looking at something and I wondered what it was. I just didn't think or I would have known.

"There you are, my good old friend," Grandpa said.

"Who is his friend, Mom?" I asked.

Mom didn't say anything. Then I saw.

"He's playin' with that old terrapin, Mom," I said.

"I know he is," Mom said.

"The terrapin doesn't mind if Grandpa strokes his head with his hand," I said.

"I know it," Mom said.

"But the old terrapin won't let me do it," I said. "Why does he let Grandpa?"

"The terrapin knows your Grandpa."

"He ought to know me," I said, "but when I try to stroke his head with my hand, he closes up in his shell."

Mom didn't say anything. She stood by the window watching Grandpa and listening to Grandpa talk to the terrapin.

"My old friend, how do you like the sunshine?" Grandpa asked the terrapin.

The terrapin turned his fleshless face to one side like a hen does when she looks at you in the sunlight. He was trying to talk to Grandpa; maybe the terrapin could understand what Grandpa was saying.

"Old fellow, it's been a hard winter," Grandpa said. "How have you fared under the smokehouse floor?"

"Does the terrapin know what Grandpa is sayin'?" I asked Mom.

"I don't know," she said.

"I'm awfully glad to see you, old fellow," Grandpa said.

He didn't offer to bite Grandpa's big soft hand as he stroked his head.

"Looks like the terrapin would bite Grandpa," I said.

"That terrapin has spent the winters under that smoke-house for fifteen years," Mom said. "Pap has been acquainted with him for eleven years. He's been talkin' to that terrapin every spring."

"How does Grandpa know the terrapin is old?" I asked Mom.

"It's got 1847 cut on its shell," Mom said. "We know he's ninety-five years old. He's older than that. We don't know how old he was when that date was cut on his back."

"Who cut 1847 on his back, Mom?"

"I don't know, child," she said, "but I'd say whoever cut that date on his back has long been under the ground."

Then I wondered how a terrapin could get that old and what kind of a looking person he was who cut the date on the terrapin's back. I wondered where it happened—if it happened near where our house stood. I wondered who lived here on this land then, what kind of a house they lived in, and if they had a sassafras with tiny thin April leaves on its top growing in their yard, and if the person that cut that date on the terrapin's back was buried at Plum Grove, if he had farmed these hills where we lived today and cut timber like Grandpa had—and if he had seen the Aprils pass like Grandpa had seen them and if he enjoyed them like Grandpa was enjoying this April. I wondered if he had looked at the dogwood blossoms, the redbud blossoms, and talked to this same terrapin.

"Are you well, old fellow?" Grandpa asked the terrapin.

The terrapin just looked at Grandpa.

"I'm well as common for a man of my age," Grandpa said.

"Did the terrapin ask Grandpa if he was well?" I asked Mom.

"I don't know," Mom said. "I can't talk to a terrapin."

"But Grandpa can."

"Yes."

"Wait until tomatoes get ripe and we'll go to the garden together," Grandpa said.

"Does the terrapin eat tomatoes?" I asked Mom.

"Yes, that terrapin has been eatin' tomatoes from our garden for fifteen years," Mom said. "When Mick was tossin' the terrapins out of the tomato patch, he picked up this one and found the date cut on his back. He put him back in the patch and told him to help himself. He lives from our garden every year. We don't bother him and don't allow anybody else to bother him. He spends his winters under our smokehouse floor buried in the dry ground."

"Gee, Grandpa looks like the terrapin," I said.

Mom didn't say anything; tears came to her eyes. She wiped them from her eyes with the corner of her apron.

"I'll be back to see you," Grandpa said. "I'm a-gettin' a little chilly; I'll be gettin' back to the house."

The terrapin twisted his wrinkled neck without moving his big body, poking his head deeper into the April wind as Grandpa pulled his bundled body up by holding to the sassafras tree trunk.

"Good-by, old friend!"

The terrapin poked his head deeper into the wind, holding one eye on Grandpa, for I could see his eye shining in the sinking sunlight.

Grandpa got his cane that was leaned against the sassafras tree trunk and hobbled slowly toward the house. The terrapin looked at him with first one eye and then the other.

REVIEWING AND INTERPRETING

Record your answers to these questions in your personal literature notebook. Follow the directions for each part.

REVIEWING Try to complete each of these sentences without looking back at the selection.

Recalling Facts

1. The old friend that Grandpa is going to visit is
   a. a terrapin.
   b. a neighbor.
   c. a bumblebee.
   d. one of the hogs.

Understanding Main Ideas

2. Both the terrapin and Grandpa
   a. are unhappy.
   b. regret growing older.
   c. enjoy being alive and seeing spring.
   d. would rather be alone.

Identifying Sequence

3. Which of the following events took place first?
   a. Mom told the boy to leave Grandpa alone.
   b. Grandpa examines a butterfly cocoon.
   c. Mom put on Grandpa's gloves.
   d. Grandpa talks to the terrapin.

Getting Meaning from Context

4. "Grandpa toddled along the path better than my baby brother could." The word *toddled* means
   a. walked with short, unsteady steps.
   b. walked very quickly.
   c. skipped along.
   d. took long strides.

Finding Supporting Details

5. Grandpa did not look exactly like Santa Claus because
   a. he was taller.
   b. he was much heavier.
   c. he did not laugh.
   d. his cheeks were different.

INTERPRETING

To complete these items, you may look back at the selection if you'd like.

Making Inferences

6. Grandpa lives with Mom because he
   a. is lonely.
   b. needs someone to take care of him.
   c. wants to be near the terrapin.
   d. wants to be near his grandson.

Generalizing

7. Grandpa can best be described as
   a. proud.
   b. silly.
   c. unhappy.
   d. unfriendly.

Recognizing Fact and Opinion

8. Which of the following is a statement of opinion?
   a. Grandpa was hard of hearing.
   b. Grandpa stopped under a pine tree.
   c. No man could lift the end of a bigger saw log than Grandpa could.
   d. Grandpa's walks get shorter each spring.

Identifying Cause and Effect

9. The terrapin lets Grandpa stroke him because the
   a. cold weather has made the terrapin move slowly.
   b. terrapin is friendly with everyone.
   c. terrapin can't pull his head into the shell.
   d. terrapin knows and trusts Grandpa.

Drawing Conclusions　　**10.** Mom cries at the end of the story because she

    a. knows that Grandpa is getting older and weaker.

    b. does not like spring.

    c. knows the terrapin will destroy the garden.

    d. does not want her son to bother Grandpa.

Now check your answers with your teacher. Study the items you answered incorrectly. What skills are they checking? Talk to your teacher about ways to work on those skills.

Use of Language

Narrative writing is writing that tells a story. Narratives may be either fiction or nonfiction. Fictional narratives are stories about imaginary people, places, and events. Nonfictional narratives are "true stories." All narratives have the same elements—characters, plot, and setting.

Nonfictional narratives share another characteristic with fiction—the author chooses a point of view from which he or she tells the story. In "Another April" Stuart is the first-person narrator telling the story about his grandfather. When a story is written as if one of the characters is telling it, it is being told from the *first person point of view*, and the author uses *I* or *me* when that character is speaking.

After deciding from which point of view to tell the story, the author decides how best to help readers, to "experience" the story. The author wants them to see, hear, and feel what the characters see, hear, and feel. When we read "Another April," Stuart wants us to do more than just read the words. He wants us to *see* the family farm in Kentucky and Grandpa toddling along the path like a small child. He wants us to *hear* Grandpa's voice and to *feel* the cool wind against Grandpa's face. Stuart tries to accomplish this by means of the language—the way he chooses and arranges words.

In the lessons that follow you will learn about three ways that authors use language to help you experience the events in a story.

1. **Using Dialect**   People in different parts of the United States have different ways of speaking. A way of speaking that is typical of one part of the country is called *dialect*. Authors use dialect to make a story seem more authentic, or real. They have the characters speak in the same dialect as that of people who live in that region.

2. **Using Descriptive Words**   Authors choose their words carefully to give readers a clear picture of the people, places, and things they describe. The use of colorful adjectives and strong verbs helps writers create vivid images.

3. **Using Figurative Language**   Authors sometimes use words or phrases in unusual ways to help readers picture the people, places, and things they are describing. They may use words or phrases with meanings that are different from their ordinary, or literal meanings. When authors use language in this way, they are using *figurative language.*

LESSON 1   **USING DIALECT**

Even among people who speak the same language—English, for example—no two people speak in exactly the same way. Despite some individual differences, people who live together in one particular part or region of the country tend to speak in a similar way. Any difference in the way of speaking that distinguishes one such group from another is called *dialect*. For example, people who live in and around Boston, Massachusetts, tend to speak in a similar way, and people who live in the area of New Orleans, Louisiana, tend to speak in another way.

As you read "Another April," did you notice anything unusual about the way the characters spoke? The way Grandpa, his daughter, and his grandson spoke is characteristic of the way some people speak in the region of eastern Kentucky where they lived. Stuart was very familiar with the dialect spoken in that part of the country because he lived there most of his life. He was very familiar with spoken expressions such as "I'll be a-goin' to see 'im" (I'll be going to see him). Because of his familiarity with the dialect, Stuart chose to include dialogue in his essay. *Dialogue* is the actual conversation between characters.

Read this passage from the selection. Notice Stuart's use of dialect in the conversation between Grandpa and Mom.

> "Now, Pap, you won't get cold," Mom said as she put a heavy wool cap over his head.
>
> "Huh, what did ye say?" Grandpa asked, holding his big hand cupped over his ear to catch the sound.
>
> "Wait until I get your gloves," Mom said, hollering real loud in Grandpa's ear. Mom had forgotten about his gloves until he raised his big bare hand above his ear to catch the sound of Mom's voice.
>
> "Don't get 'em," Grandpa said. "I won't ketch cold."

What examples of dialect did you find in Grandpa's speech? Did you notice that he used "ye" for *you*, " 'em" for *them*, and "ketch" for *catch*? Throughout the selection Stuart has all of his characters speak in dialect. The grandson (Stuart) uses expressions such as: "[Grandpa] *quarreled at* Mom" and "[Grandpa would] take me on his knee and tell me about *all what* he had seen." Mom says such things as "Before you's born" and "he quit cuttin' timber and farmin'." These expressions are examples of the dialect of the area where the family lives.

Although the English and grammar used by Stuart's characters in "Another April" would not be considered proper in other parts of the country, they are perfectly understandable in the region where the characters live because that is the dialect spoken there. Stuart wants you to "hear" how the characters in the story speak, because their speech accurately reflects who they are and where they live.

EXERCISE 1

Read the following passages from the selection. Use what you have learned in this lesson to help you answer the questions.

"Who is Grandpa goin' to see, Mom?" I asked.
"He's not goin' to see anybody," Mom said.
"I heard 'im say that he was goin' to see an old friend," I told her.
"Oh, he was just a-talkin'," Mom said.

"What's Grandpa doin'?" I asked Mom.
But Mom didn't answer me.
"How long has Grandpa been with us?" I asked Mom.
"Before you's born," she said. "Pap has been with us eleven years. He was eighty when he quit cuttin' timber and farmin'; now he's ninety-one."

1. What words or phrases in this passage demonstrate the dialect spoken in the part of the country where this story is set?

2. After each word or phrase you wrote in answering question 1, write how it would be said in the dialect of your part of the country.

Now check your answers with your teacher. Review this lesson if you don't understand why an answer was incorrect.

WRITING ON YOUR OWN 1

In this exercise you will use what you learned in lesson 1 to write three or four paragaphs describing a memorable personal experience. Your paragraphs should include some dialect. Follow these steps:

- Review your list of personal experiences and the brief notes you wrote about each for Writing: Developing a Nonfictional Narrative.
- Choose as the subject of your narrative the experience that you think would be of the most interest to other people.
- Using your notes to help you get started, write three or four paragraphs describing your experience. Include some dialogue (conversation). Try to include some dialect that is typical of the area where you live. Dialect may include words and expressions that are common only to your area or perhaps only to your age group.
- Remember to enclose dialogue in quotation marks.

LESSON 2   USING DESCRIPTIVE WORDS

Like artists, good writers paint pictures. Instead of using paints to create images on canvas, however, writers use words to create images on paper. The more precise, lively, and colorful the writer's words are, the more vivid the images, or word pictures, become that he or she paints.

Good writers like to use colorful adjectives and strong verbs. Read this passage from the selection and notice how Stuart has carefully chosen certain adjectives and verbs to help create a vivid picture for you.

As I watched Grandpa go down the path toward the hog pen, he stopped to examine every little thing along his path. Once he waved his cane at a butterfly as it zigzagged over his head, its polka-dot wings fanning the blue April air.

What words does Stuart use to describe the butterfly's wings and the way in which the butterfly flew over Grandpa's head? To create a vivid picture of the butterfly, Stuart uses the colorful adjective *polka-dot* and the verb *fanning* to describe its wings. Instead of using a weak verb such as *flew*, Stuart chooses the strong verb *zigzagged* to describe the manner in which the butterfly flew.

Notice the verb Stuart uses in the following passage to describe how Grandpa walked.

Mom stood watching Grandpa too. I think she was afraid that he would fall. But Mom was fooled; Grandpa toddled along the path better than my baby brother could.

Stuart could have said "Grandpa walked or strolled along the path," but instead he uses the specific verb *toddled* to describe how he walked. The word *toddle* means "to walk with short, unsteady steps, as a baby does." Stuart deliberately uses *toddled* because he wants readers to understand and see that Grandpa—once a strong, powerful man—at 91 years old has become so unsteady on his feet that he resembles a young child learning to walk.

EXERCISE 2

Read this passage from the selection. Use what you have learned in this lesson to answer the questions that follow it.

The terrapin twisted his wrinkled neck without moving his big body, poking his head deeper into the April wind as Grandpa pulled his bundled body up by holding to the sassafras tree trunk.

"Good-by, old friend!"

The terrapin poked his head deeper into the wind, holding one eye on Grandpa, for I could see his eye shining in the sinking sunlight.

Grandpa got his cane that was leaned against the sassafras tree trunk and hobbled slowly toward the house. The terrapin looked at him with first one eye and then the other.

1. What descriptive adjectives does Stuart use in the passage?

2. What strong, descriptive verbs does Stuart use in the passage?

Now check your answers with your teacher. Review this lesson if you don't understand why an answer was incorrect.

WRITING ON YOUR OWN 2

In this exercise you will use what you have learned in this lesson to add colorful adjectives and strong verbs to your description of a personal experience.

- Reread the paragraphs you wrote for Writing on Your Own 1. Have you used colorful adjectives and strong verbs to describe the people, places, events, and actions that you tell about?
- Underline the adjectives and verbs that you think could be replaced with more-descriptive words. Ask yourself what different words you could use that would help to create a

more vivid picture for the readers. Use a dictionary or a thesaurus to help you find more-colorful adjectives and stronger verbs.

• Now rewrite your paragraphs, substituting words that are more colorful and descriptive.

LESSON 3 — USING FIGURATIVE LANGUAGE

Figurative language refers to words or phrases used in unusual ways to create strong, vivid images; to focus attention on certain ideas; or to compare unlike things. Authors use figurative language to help readers see things that are ordinary or familiar in new and more interesting ways.

Figurative language uses figures of speech. *Figures of speech* are words or phrases used in ways other than their ordinary, or literal, meanings to create vivid images. For example, if you read: "The lush grass was a green carpet spread across the field," you would know that the writer did not literally mean that the grass was a green carpet. He or she was comparing the grass covering the field to a green carpet in order to create a vivid picture.

There are several types of figures of speech. In this lesson we will examine the three most common: simile, metaphor, and personification.

Simile   How often do you make comparisons when you speak? Probably more than you realize. Sometimes it's the easiest way to describe something or to suggest a feeling. Have you ever used or heard these expressions: "a mind like a computer," "as white as a sheet," "a voice like a bird's"? These comparisons are called similes. A *simile* is a direct comparison between two things that are basically unlike but have some quality in common. The two things are connected by the word *like*, *as*, or *than*, or a verb such as *appears* or *seems*.

Stuart uses similes throughout "Another April." His love of nature is clear in his use of vivid comparisons. Read the following passage. As you read, notice how Stuart describes Grandpa's laugh.

> "Yer Ma's a-puttin' enough clothes on me to kill a man," Grandpa said; then he laughed a coarse laugh like March wind among the pine tops at his own words. I started laughing but not at Grandpa's words. He thought I was laughing at them and we both laughed together. . . . But I was laughing at the way he was dressed.

Grandpa was a big man who used to cut timber for a living. Stuart describes his laugh as "coarse," suggesting that it sounded rough or hoarse. Stuart could have left his description at that—saying simply that it was a coarse laugh. To help readers experience, or "hear," what Grandpa's laugh sounded like, however, he compares it to a March wind blowing among the pines. If you've ever heard strong wind blowing through the tops of pine trees, you know that it produces a loud, deep roar. Stuart uses a simile to emphasize that Grandpa had a loud and powerful laugh.

Metaphor   Another kind of comparison authors use is metaphor. A *metaphor* also compares two basically unlike things, but it does so without using a word of comparison such as *like* or *as*. A metaphor suggests that one thing *is* another. For example, read the following description: "The flowers in Grandma's garden are a rainbow." The speaker does not really mean that the flowers are a rainbow. He or she means that the flowers of many different colors look like a rainbow with its many different colors.

Instead of using a simile to describe Grandpa's coarse laugh, as Stuart did in the example given ("he laughed a coarse laugh like March wind among the pine tops"), he could have written the comparison as a metaphor instead ("his coarse laugh was a March wind among the pine tops").

Personification   Another effective figure of speech is personification. *Personification* is a figure of speech in which an animal, an object, or an idea is given human characteristics or qualities. Its use can add life to a piece of writing by helping readers view common things in a new way. "The wind came dancing down from the mountain and knocked gently at my door" is an example of personification. We know that the wind cannot really dance or knock on a door. By personifying the wind, the writer is giving readers a stronger image, a better picture, of what the wind was like. Writers and cartoonists create wonderful characters by giving animals voices and a personalities. Snoopy is not just a dog in *Peanuts*, for example, nor is Charlotte just a spider in *Charlotte's Web*. They are both intelligent, thinking creatures. These nonhuman characters take on human qualities through the use of personification.

Read this passage from the selection. Look for Stuart's use of personification in it.

> As I watched Grandpa go down the path toward the hog pen, he stopped to examine every little thing along his path. Once he waved his cane at a butterfly as it zigzagged over his head, its polka-dot wings fanning the blue air. Grandpa would stand when a puff of wind came along, and hold his face against the wind and let the wind play with his white whiskers. I thought maybe his face was hot under his beard and he was letting the wind cool his face.

Did you find the personification "let the wind play with his white whiskers"? By describing the wind as "playing," Stuart has personified it.

EXERCISE 3

Read these two passages from the selection. Use what you have learned in this lesson to answer the questions that follow them.

> Grandpa was wearing a heavy wool suit that hung loosely about his big body but fitted him tightly round the waist where he was as big and as round as a flour barrel. His pant legs were as big 'round his pipestem legs as emptied meal sacks. And his big shoes, with his heavy wool socks dropping down over their tops, looked like sled runners. Grandpa wore a heavy wool shirt and over his wool shirt he wore a heavy wool sweater and then his coat over the top of all this. Over his coat he wore a heavy overcoat and about his neck he wore a wool scarf.

> I had heard her tell how he'd sweat and how the sweat of his beard would be icicles by the time he got home from work on the cold winter days. Now Mom wouldn't let him get out of the house, for she wanted him to live for a long time.

1. What kind of figure of speech does Stuart use in the first passage? What two basically unlike things does he compare? In what ways does he mean the two things are alike?

2. What kind of figure of speech does Stuart use in the second passage? What two basically unlike things does he compare? In what way does he mean the two things are alike?

Now check your answers with your teacher. Review this lesson if you don't understand why an answer was incorrect.

WRITING ON YOUR OWN 3

In this exercise you will use what you have learned in this lesson to add figures of speech to your description of a personal experience.

- Reread the revised paragraphs you wrote for Writing on Your Own 2. As you read, try to think of some unusual comparisons using a simile or a metaphor that will help your readers experience what you saw, heard, touched, tasted, or smelled.
- Think about adding personification to your description. Is there some description that seems vague or uninteresting? See whether you can give it some life by lending it some human quality or characteristic. For example, if you were describing an enjoyable camping trip in the forest that you didn't want to end, you might say, "The forest captured us and wouldn't let us go."
- Now rewrite your paragraphs to include these figures of speech.

DISCUSSION GUIDES

1. In the beginning of the story, the author describes Grandpa as *toddling* along the path. In the last paragraph of the story, however, Grandpa "*hobbled* slowly toward the house." In a small group, discuss why the author uses *hobbled* at the end of the story. What is the difference between *toddled* and *hobbled?* How does the word choice affect your picture of Grandpa? Share your opinions with the rest of the class.

2. Discuss with your classmates why Grandpa considers the terrapin a friend. Why does he want to visit him every spring? What do they have in common?

3. With a partner make up some dialogue for the terrapin. What do you think he would like to ask or say to Grandpa? Refer to the story and find the places where Grandpa asks the terrapin questions. Then write what you and your partner think the terrapin might answer. Share your dialogue with the rest of the class.

WRITE A NONFICTIONAL NARRATIVE

In this unit you have seen how Stuart uses language to create vivid images of the people, places, and events he describes in his nonfictional narrative "Another April."

Follow these steps to complete your narrative essay. If you have questions about the writing process, refer to Using the Writing Process (page 217).

* Gather and review the following pieces of writing you did for this unit: 1) a list of personal experiences and brief notes describing highlights of each, from Writing: Developing a Nonfictional Narrative; 2) paragraphs describing the experience, including dialect, from Writing on Your Own 1; 3) paragraphs revised with stronger descriptive words, from Writing on Your Own 2; 4) paragraphs revised with figures of speech, from Writing on Your Own 3.

* Write a title and a short introductory paragraph for your narrative. Try to catch the attention and interest of your readers so that they will want to read about your personal experience.

* Reread the paragraphs you wrote for Writing on Your Own 3 to be sure you have given an accurate and vivid description of your experience. When you are satisfied that your description will give your readers a clear picture of your experience, add these paragraphs to your introductory paragraph.

* Finish your story. Write several more paragraphs. Remember to use colorful adjectives to describe your characters and strong verbs to describe the action. Also when your characters speak, be sure to write in the dialect they would actually use.

* Ask a classmate to read your narrative and make suggestions for improvement. If you think the suggestions are good ones, use them to revise your writing.

- Proofread your narrative for errors in spelling, grammar, punctuation, and capitalization. Then make a final copy and save it in your writing portfolio.
- If time permits, read your narrative to a group or the whole class. If your story has a lot of dialogue between characters, you may wish to have a partner read one character's lines.

Author's Purpose

How to Improve
Your Vocabulary

by Tony Randall

INTRODUCTION

BUILDING
BACKGROUND

Did you know that the English language is spoken by more than 350 million people? It is spoken by more people than any other language in the world except Chinese. In many ways English has become the international language. It is used more than any other language for international communication in such fields as business, politics, science, and even entertainment.

English already has a larger vocabulary than any other language, and it's growing every day. Because of advances in science, technology, and other fields, more new words and more new meanings for old words are continually being added to the language.

It is not possible to learn all of the words in the English vocabulary, but as you will learn in Tony Randall's "How to Improve Your Vocabulary," the more words that you know and can use correctly in your speech and writing, the greater your chances for attaining success in this world. In his article Randall tells how he has acquired an enormous vocabulary and teaches readers how to build a large one too.

The English language includes more than 1 million words. Reading a wide variety of fiction and nonfiction books is a good way to add some of those words to your vocabulary.

ABOUT THE AUTHOR

Tony Randall was born Leonard Rosenberg in Tulsa, Oklahoma, in 1920. He has gained fame as an accomplished actor, appearing in films, on television, and in plays on Broadway. He is probably best known for his role as Felix Unger in the television series *The Odd Couple*. His acting ability has won him many awards, but Randall has many other interests. He started the National Actors Theatre in New York City and has written two books about the theater and life as an actor. He loves opera, classical music, and paintings. Randall also has another love—words. In fact, his love and knowledge of words serve him well as an advisor on word usage for the *American Heritage Dictionary*.

ABOUT THE LESSONS

The lessons that follow "How to Improve Your Vocabulary" focus on the author's purpose for writing. Authors of nonfiction may write to inform, to instruct, to persuade, or to entertain. When an author has more than one purpose for writing, one of those purposes is usually more important than the others.

In these lessons you will learn about the different purposes nonfiction writers have and about how they accomplish those purposes.

WRITING: DEVELOPING AN INSTRUCTIONAL ARTICLE

At the end of this unit, you will write an instructional article. The following suggestions will help you get started:

- The title of your article will be "How to Find Information in an Encyclopedia." There are several types of encyclopedias. You will write your article about the one used most commonly—the general encyclopedia.
- Your purpose for writing will be to instruct your readers about how to find information in an encyclopedia.

- Begin by gathering some facts about the encyclopedia. You can find such facts right in an encyclopedia or in other reference books that can be found in the library.
- Write a list of 6 to 10 facts about the encyclopedia. Include a definition of *encyclopedia* and a few facts about its history. Choose interesting facts that you think your readers may enjoy learning. For example, readers might be interested to learn that the word *encyclopedia* comes from the Greek words *enkyklios paideia* meaning "circular (well-rounded) education."
- To help organize your notes, make a copy of the graphic organizer below. Under the heading "What an Encyclopedia Is," write your definition of *encyclopedia*.
- Under the heading "Interesting Facts About the Encyclopedia," list the remaining facts you found.
- Save your graphic organizer. You will need it for the next lesson.

What an Encyclopedia Is

Interesting Facts About the Encyclopedia

How to Find a Topic in an Encyclopedia

Why It's Important to Know How to Use an Encyclopedia

AS YOU
READ

Think about these questions as you read "How to Improve Your Vocabulary." They will help you identify Tony Randall's purpose for writing it.

- Does the author just give you information in the article?
- Does the author teach you anything? If so, what?
- Are you entertained by anything the author wrote?
- What do you think is the author's main purpose for writing the article?

How to Improve Your Vocabulary

■

by Tony Randall

Words can make us laugh, cry, go to war, fall in love.

Rudyard Kipling[1] called words the most powerful drug of mankind. If they are, I'm a hopeless addict, and I hope to get you hooked, too.

Whether you're still in school or you head up a corporation, the better command you have of words, the better chance you have of saying exactly what you mean, of understanding what others mean, and of getting what you want in the world.

English is the richest language—with the largest vocabulary on earth. Over one million words. *You* can express shades of meaning that aren't even possible in other languages. For example, you can differentiate[2] between *sky* and *heaven*. The French, Italians, and Spanish cannot.

Yet the average adult has a vocabulary of only thirty thousand to sixty thousand words. Imagine what we're missing!

---

[1] English author (1865–1936)

[2] to show a difference in; to see the difference between

Here are five pointers that help me learn—and remember—whole families of words at a time. They may not look easy, and won't be at first, but if you stick with them, you'll find they work.

What's the first thing to do when you see a word you don't know?

1. Try to Guess the Meaning of the Word from the Way It's Used

You can often get at least part of a word's meaning just from how it's used in a sentence.

That's why it's so important to read as much as you can—different kinds of things: magazines, books, newspapers you don't normally read. The more you expose yourself to new words, the more words you'll pick up just by seeing how they're used.

For instance, say you run across the word *manacle*:

"The manacles had been on John's wrists for thirty years. Only one person had a key: his wife."

You have a good idea of what *manacles* are, just from the context of the sentence.

But let's find out exactly what the word means and where it comes from. The only way to do this, and to build an extensive vocabulary fast, is to go to the dictionary. (How lucky that you can; Shakespeare couldn't. There wasn't an English dictionary in his day.)

So you go to the dictionary. (**Note:** Don't let dictionary abbreviations put you off. Up front you'll find what they mean. You'll also find a guide to pronunciation symbols there, as well as an abbreviated version on each page.)

2. Look It Up

Here's the definition for *manacle* in *The American Heritage Dictionary of the English Language*.

man·a·cle (măn'ə-kəl) *n.* Usually plural. **1.** A device for confining the hands, usually consisting of two metal rings that are fastened about the wrists and joined by a metal chain; a handcuff. **2.** Anything that confines or restrains.—*tr. v.* **manacled, -cling, -cles. 1.** To restrain with manacles. **2.** To confine or restrain as if with manacles; shackle; fetter. [Middle English *manicle*, from Old French, from Latin *manicula*, little hand, handle, diminutive of *manus*, hand. See **man-** in Appendix.[3]*]

The first definition fits here: "a device for confining the hands, usually consisting of two metal rings that are fastened about the wrists and joined by a metal chain; a handcuff."

Well, that's what you *thought* it meant. But what's the idea behind the word? What are its roots? To really understand a word, you need to know.

Here's where the detective work—and the fun—begins.

3. Dig the Meaning Out by the Roots

The root is the basic part of the word—its heritage, its origin. Most roots in English come from Latin and Greek words at least two thousand years old, which come from even earlier IndoEuropean[4] tongues.

Learning the roots: (1) helps us remember words; (2) gives us a deeper understanding of the words we already know; and (3) allows us to pick up whole families of new words at a time. That's why learning the root is the most important part of going to the dictionary.

Notice that the root of *manacle* is *manus* (Latin), meaning "hand."

---

[3] additional material or information at the end of a book

[4] a family of languages that includes most of those spoken in Europe and many of those spoken in southwestern Asia and India

Well, that makes sense. Now other words with this root, *man*, start to make sense, too.

Take *manual*—something done "by hand" (*manual* labor) or a "handbook." And *manage*—to "handle" something (as a *manager*). When you *emancipate* someone, you're taking him "from the hands of" someone else.

When you *manufacture* something, you "make it by hand" (in its original meaning).

And when you finish your first novel, your publisher will see your (originally "handwritten") *manuscript*.

Imagine! A whole new world of words opens up—just from one simple root.

The root gives the basic clue to the meaning of a word. But there's another important clue that runs a close second: the *prefix*.

4. Get the Powerful Prefixes Under Your Belt

A prefix is the part that's sometimes attached to the front of a word, such as—well, "*prefix*." There aren't many—less than a hundred major prefixes—and you'll learn them in no time at all just by becoming more aware of the meanings of words you already know. Here are a few. (Some of the vocabulary-building how-to books will give you the others.)

PREFIX		MEANING	EXAMPLES	
(*Lat.*)	(*Gk.*)			(*Literal sense*)
com, con,	sym, syn	with, very,	conform	(form with)
co, col, cor	syl	together	sympathy	(feeling with)
in, im,	a, an	not,	innocent	(not wicked)
il, ir		without	amorphus	(without form)
contra,	anti,	against,	contravene	(come against)
counter	ant	opposite	antidote	(give against)

Now see how the prefix (along with the context) helps you get the meaning of the italicized words:

"If you're going to be my witness, your story must _corroborate_ my story." (The literal meaning of _corroborate_ is "strength together.")

"First you told me one thing—now you tell me another. Don't _contradict_ yourself." The literal meaning of _contradict_ is "say against."

"Oh, that snake's not poisonous. It's a completely _innocuous_ little garden snake." The literal meaning of _innocuous_ is "not harmful."

Now you've got some new words. What are you going to do with them?

5. Put Your New Words to Work at Once

Use them several times the first day you learn them. Say them out loud. Write them in sentences.

Should you "use" them on friends? Careful. You don't want them to think you're a stuffed shirt. It depends on the situation. You know when a word sounds natural and when it sounds stuffy.

How about your enemies? You have my blessing. Ask one of them if he's read that article on pneumonoultramicroscopicsilicovolcanoconiosis. (You really can find it in the dictionary.) Now you're one up on him.

So what do you do to improve your vocabulary?

Remember: (1) Try to guess the meaning of the word from the way it's used; (2) look it up; (3) dig the meaning out by the roots; (4) get the powerful prefixes under your belt; (5) put your new words to work at once.

That's all there is to it. You're off on your treasure hunt.

Now do you see why I love words so much?

Aristophanes[5] said, "By words, the mind is excited and the spirit elated." It's as true today as it was when he said it in Athens—twenty-four hundred years ago.

I hope you're now like me—hooked on words forever.

---

[5] 448?–380? B.C.; a very famous Greek writer of comic plays

REVIEWING AND INTERPRETING

Record your answers to these questions in your personal literature notebook. Follow the directions for each part.

REVIEWING   Try to complete each of these sentences without looking back at the selection.

Recalling Facts

1. The language with the largest vocabulary is
   a. Italian.
   b. Greek.
   c. Spanish.
   d. English.

Understanding Main Ideas

2. The greatest benefit of having a large vocabulary is that it enables a speaker or writer to
   a. better understand and be understood by others.
   b. impress friends.
   c. speak other languages.
   d. write poetry.

Identifying Sequence

3. The first step in finding out what an unfamiliar word means is to
   a. look for a prefix.
   b. look it up in the dictionary.
   c. guess what the root of the word is.
   d. try to figure out the word's meaning from how it is used.

Finding Supporting Details

4. The author says that we are luckier than Shakespeare because
   a. no one spoke English when he lived.
   b. he did not have a dictionary.
   c. he did not have magazines or newspapers.
   d. he did not understand the origins of words.

Getting Meaning from Context

5. Aristophanes said, "By words, the mind is excited and the spirit elated." The word *elated* means
  a. worried.
  b. joyful.
  c. depressed.
  d. doubtful.

INTERPRETING

To complete these items, you may look back at the selection if you'd like.

Making Inferences

6. In the article, the author expresses the belief that
  a. there are too many words in the English language.
  b. the average adult's vocabulary is large enough.
  c. the average adult's vocabulary is small when compared with the total number of words in the English language.
  d. the English language has borrowed too many words from other languages.

Generalizing

7. The author's feeling about learning new words can best be described as
  a. excited.
  b. disappointed.
  c. confused.
  d. uninterested.

Recognizing Fact and Opinion

8. Which of the following is a statement of opinion?
  a. A prefix is the part that is sometimes attached to the front of a word.
  b. The root is the basic part of the word.
  c. Dictionaries often give the origin of a word.
  d. Words are the most powerful drug of mankind.

Identifying Cause and Effect

9. According to the author, English is the richest language in the world because
   a. most people speak English.
   b. it has the largest vocabulary in the world.
   c. it has so many verbs.
   d. it is the only language that has a dictionary.

Drawing Conclusions

10. From this article, you can conclude that the author
   a. wants to write his own dictionary.
   b. feels that we need to know only about 30 thousand words.
   c. finds words exciting and enjoys learning new ones.
   d. feels that a good dictionary is all we need to learn new words.

Now check your answers with your teacher. Study the items you answered incorrectly. What skills are they checking? Talk with your teacher about ways to work on those skills.

Author's Purpose

Author's purpose is the reason an author has for writing. As you learned in Unit 1, authors sometimes have more than one reason or purpose for writing a particular work, although one purpose is usually the most important.

Authors of nonfiction may have one or more of the following purposes: to give information, to teach how to do something, to entertain, to express an opinion, or to persuade readers to do or believe something.

Do you think Tony Randall had more than one purpose in mind when he wrote "How to Improve Your Vocabulary"? You're right if you think he did. For what purposes do you think Randall wrote the article?

In the lessons that follow we will examine Randall's purposes for writing his article and how he tried to achieve those purposes:

1. **Author's Purpose: To Inform and to Instruct** When an author's purpose is to inform, he or she gives information about a specific subject. Instruction is a special kind of information. When an author's purpose is to instruct, he or she tells the reader how to do or make something.

2. **Author's Purpose: To Persuade and to Entertain** When an author's purpose is to persuade, he or she presents arguments or reasons in order to persuade the reader to accept his or her view or opinion about a subject. Regardless of what other purpose or purposes an author may have for writing a particular piece of non-fiction, the author wants the writing to entertain the reader.

3. **Author's Purpose and Organization** Most articles begin with a lead paragraph that is meant to capture the reader's attention and let the reader know what the author

is going to write about. The author then must organize the information that follows in a way that the reader can understand. One device an author may use to help organize information is subheads—short titles within the article that identify the beginning of each new topic.

LESSON 1 — AUTHOR'S PURPOSE: TO INFORM AND TO INSTRUCT

You discovered while reading "How to Improve Your Vocabulary," that Tony Randall had more than one purpose for writing the article. One of his purposes is to provide some information about the English language and its vocabulary.

Read this passage from the article. As you read, think about the information Randall presents.

> English is the richest language—with the largest vocabulary on earth. Over one million words. *You* can express shades of meaning that aren't even possible in other languages. For example, you can differentiate between *sky* and *heaven*. The French, Italians, and Spanish cannot.
>
> Yet the average adult has a vocabulary of only thirty thousand to sixty thousand words. Imagine what we're missing!

Randall gives several interesting facts in this passage. He tells readers that English has the largest vocabulary on earth, more than one million words; that English can express shades of meaning that aren't even possible in other languages; and that the average adult has a vocabulary of only 30 thousand to 60 thousand words.

When you read factual information such as Randall gives, you need to consider whether the facts are correct.

Usually, you can assume that any information an author presents is accurate unless you have some reason to suspect the author's motives for writing or believe that the author may have been careless in gathering the facts. Because facts can be proved and false statements disproved, you can usually check their accuracy in an encyclopedia or other good reference source. Some authors give their sources of information within the article.

As interesting as the facts are, giving information was not Randall's main purpose for writing the article. His most important purpose was to instruct—to teach a strategy for improving your vocabulary. He makes this purpose clear in this passage from the article:

> Here are five pointers that help me learn—and remember—whole families of words at a time. They may not look easy, and won't be at first, but if you stick with them, you'll find they work.

Randall then goes on to teach his five-step strategy for improving vocabulary. There are three standards we can use to judge instructions. First, they should be clear. They should tell readers exactly what to do in clear, easy-to-understand language. Second, they should be complete, not leaving out any steps. Third, the steps should be given in the correct order. Do you think Randall's instructions meet these standards?

EXERCISE 1

Read these two passages from the article. Use what you have learned from this lesson to answer the questions that follow them.

But let's find out exactly what the word means and where it comes from. The only way to do this, and to build an extensive vocabulary fast, is to go to the dictionary. (How lucky that you can; Shakespeare couldn't. There wasn't an English dictionary in his day.)

The root is the basic part of the word—its heritage, its origin. Most roots in English come from Latin and Greek words at least two thousand years old, which come from even earlier Indo-European tongues.

1. In which passage, the first or the second, does Randall give information and instruction? Explain your answer.

2. What facts does Randall include in these two passages?

Now check your answers with your teacher. Review this lesson if you don't understand why an answer was incorrect.

 WRITING ON YOUR OWN 1

In this exercise you will use what you have learned in this lesson to begin to develop instructions telling how to find information in an encyclopedia. Follow these steps:

- Think about ways to explain how to find information in an encyclopedia about a particular topic. You should explain that the volumes (books) in an encyclopedia are arranged in alphabetical order; that each volume has a guide letter or letters and a number on its spine; and that the guide letter or letters identify the beginning letter of all of the main topics in that volume.
- Explain how to choose a key word to look for. For example, suppose the readers need to answer the question "How are clouds formed?" They should look for the key

word *clouds.* You should explain that to find information about a person, one must use the person's last name as the key word.

- Explain how the guide word or guide words at the top of each page can help readers find the page on which information on their topic begins.
- Now, under the heading "How to Find a Topic in an Encyclopedia" in your graphic organizer, write a first draft of your instructions.
- Save your graphic organizer. You will need it for the next lesson.

LESSON 2

AUTHOR'S PURPOSE: TO PERSUADE AND TO ENTERTAIN

Besides giving some information about the English language and teaching an effective strategy to improve vocabulary, Randall also has another purpose. He wants to persuade others to believe as he does—that no matter who readers are or what they do, acquiring a large vocabulary greatly increases their chances for success in the world. In addition to this practical reason for acquiring a larger vocabulary, Randall also hopes to inspire a love for the study of words.

To persuade readers, Randall mentions several ways that a better vocabulary can be helpful. He also refers to two famous authors of the past whose views agree with his. One was Aristophanes, whom he quotes: "By words, the mind is excited and the spirit elated." Randall adds that Aristophanes' view of words is as true today as it was 2,400 years ago when he made the statement in Athens, Greece.

Whatever purposes authors of informative or instructive nonfiction have for writing, they want to hold the reader's interest. They know that readers expect to get some enjoyment from their reading.

Think about how Randall entertains you in "How to

Improve Your Vocabulary." One method he uses is to include interesting facts. You learned that there was no English dictionary in Shakespeare's day, that Rudyard Kipling was a lover of words, and that the Spanish, French, and Italian languages do not have separate words for *sky* or *heaven*. Were you surprised to learn that the average adult has a vocabulary of *only* 30 thousand to 60 thousand words?

Randall knows that we do not need that information to learn his strategy for improving vocabulary. He includes these facts to add to the enjoyment of reading the article.

Randall's tone also contributes to the enjoyment of reading the article. *Tone* is the writer's attitude toward his or her subject and toward the audience (the readers). Some writers are very serious in writing about their topic or subject. Others are lighter and more humorous. Randall's attitude is both serious and light. He is serious about the importance of acquiring a large vocabulary and about teaching a strategy to help improve vocabulary, but he presents his views and teaches his five-step strategy in a lighthearted, humorous way. His attitude toward the reader is relaxed and friendly, and he wants the reader to feel that way too. Did you notice that Randall talks directly to the reader, using the pronoun *you* throughout? This method helps him, the author, make a personal connection with you, the reader.

EXERCISE 2

Read this passage from the article. Use what you have learned in this lesson to answer the questions that follow it.

Rudyard Kipling called words the most powerful drug of mankind. If they are, I'm a hopeless addict, and I hope to get you hooked, too.

Whether you're still in school or you head up a corporation, the better command you have of words, the better chance you have of saying exactly what you mean, of understanding what others mean, and of getting what you want in the world.

English is the richest language—with the largest vocabulary on earth. Over one million words.

1. How does Randall try to persuade readers of the importance of increasing their knowledge of words?

2. What sentence in the passage is *not* intended to persuade readers to agree with Randall's views about the need for a large vocabulary?

 WRITING ON YOUR OWN 2

In this exercise you will use what you have learned in the lesson to write a few reasons why you believe it's important to know how to find information in an encyclopedia. Follow these steps:

- A third purpose for writing your article—to inform and to instruct are the first two—is to persuade readers that it is important to know how to locate information in an encyclopedia. Think of reasons that this is an important skill to have both in and out of school.
- Below the heading "Why It's Important to Know How to Use an Encyclopedia," list your reasons.
- Review the list of facts that you wrote in your organizer for Writing: Developing an Instructional Article. Could any new facts make your article more interesting and enjoyable? If so, add them. Remember, your fourth purpose for writing is to entertain your readers.
- Save your list. You will need it in the next lesson.

LESSON 3 **AUTHOR'S PURPOSE AND ORGANIZATION**

Once Randall decided on his purposes for writing and gathered the information he wanted to include, he had to organize the information.

Most articles begin with a lead paragraph that is meant to capture readers' interest. A *lead paragraph* is the opening paragraph of an article. Randall's lead paragraph is very short—only one sentence: "Words can make us laugh, cry, go to war, fall in love." Despite its brevity, it catches readers' attention and lets them know that the article is going to be about the power of words.

The most important purpose of Randall's article is to teach a strategy for improving vocabulary. Writing instructions is not an easy task. It takes careful thought and organization. In Lesson 1 of this unit, you learned that there are three standards to use in judging instructions: (1) they should be clear; (2) they should be complete; and (3) the steps should be given in correct order. Randall knew that it was important to explain his five-step strategy in a sensible order. To do this, he used a device of organization you learned about in Unit 1—subheads. Randall's numbered subheads clearly show the steps in correct sequence and briefly describe each step.

Read this passage from the article. It describes a step in Randall's strategy. Before you begin, turn the subhead into a question. Then see whether the information in the passage answers your question.

3. Dig the Meaning Out by the Roots

The root is the basic part of the word—its heritage, its origin. Most roots in English come from Latin and Greek words at least two thousand years old, which come from even earlier Indo-European tongues.

Learning the root: (1) helps us remember words; (2) gives us a deeper understanding of the words we already know; and (3) allows us to pick up whole families of new words at a time. That's why learning the root is the most important part of going to the dictionary.

Notice that the root of *manacle* is *manus* (Latin), meaning "hand."

Well, that makes sense. Now other words with this root, *man*, start to make sense, too.

Take *manual*—something done "by hand" (*manual* labor) or a "handbook." And *manage*—to "handle" something (as a *manager*). When you *emancipate* some-one, you're taking him "from the hands of" someone else. . . .

The root gives the basic clue to the meaning of a word.

Did you ask yourself, "*How* do I dig the meaning out by the roots?" Did the paragraphs in the passage answer the question for you? Notice Randall's clear organization in explaining this step of his strategy. First, he explains what a root is. Then he tells of three ways that learning roots can help people decode words. Finally, he gives an example to show how learning the root of a word allows readers to learn a whole family of new words.

EXERCISE 　3

1. What are the five steps in Randall's strategy for improving vocabulary? Use the subheads in the article to help you answer.

2. If you can't guess the meaning of a word from the way it is used in a sentence, what should you do next?

Now check your answers with your teacher. Review this lesson if you don't understand why an answer was incorrect.

WRITING ON YOUR OWN 3

In this exercise you will use what you learned in this lesson to organize your instructions for how to locate information in an encyclopedia. Follow these steps:

- Think about the three standards you learned for judging instructions: (1) they should be clear; (2) they should be complete; and (3) the steps should be given in the correct order.
- Review the instructions you wrote for Writing on Your Own 1. Do they meet each of the three standards?
- Check in particular to see whether the steps in your instructions are clear and are presented in the correct order. For example, be sure that you don't explain how to find the correct page in an encyclopedia before you explain how to find the correct volume.
- Consider using numbered subheads to introduce each step in the process as Randall did in "How to Improve Your Vocabulary."
- Rewrite your instructions in paragraph form.

DISCUSSION GUIDES

1. In small groups discuss why it is important to increase word power. How can a better command of words help people? What can we learn about a person from his or her vocabulary? Share your opinions with the rest of the class.

2. As a class discuss how reading "How to Improve Your Vocabulary" has influenced your attitude toward words. Randall obviously is excited about words. Did he succeed in passing some of that excitement on to you? Why or why not? Will you use his techniques the next time you see an unfamiliar word?

3. People in the United States and England speak the same language—English—yet many of the words we use in the United States are different from the words the English use to describe the same objects. For example, in England an *elevator* is called *a lift;* a *yard* is called a *garden;* and the *trunk* of a car is called a *boot.* Even in the United States, different words are used to describe the same thing. Depending on what region of the country you live in, a soft drink might be called a *soda,* a *pop,* or a *tonic;* and a *milk-shake* might be called a *frappe.* As part of a small group, do some research and find additional examples of different words used to describe the same thing. Share the list with the rest of the class.

WRITE AN INSTRUCTIONAL ARTICLE

In this unit you have learned how to develop an instructional article. Now you will use what you have learned to write your article.

Follow these steps to complete your article. If you have questions about the writing process, refer to Using the Writing Process page 217.

- Gather and review the following pieces of writing you did in this unit: 1) the definition of an encyclopedia and a list of interesting facts, 2) a first draft of your instructions for how to use an encyclopedia, 3) a list of your reasons for knowing how to use an encyclopedia, 4) your revised instructions, 5) the graphic organizer you used throughout the unit.
- After reviewing what you've written so far, you will see that you have almost all you need for your article. Begin by writing the title. Then write your lead, or opening, paragraph. Remember, the lead paragraph should attract your readers' attention. Include your definition of an encyclopedia in the opening paragraph.
- In the next paragraph or two, present the facts you think your readers will find interesting and enjoyable. Try to use a lighthearted, humorous tone in your writing.
- Next, present your instructions for how to use an encyclopedia, being sure that they meet the three standards for good instructions.
- Close your article by presenting reasons that you hope will convince your readers of the importance of knowing how to use an encyclopedia.
- Ask a partner to read your completed article, comment on the article in general and your instructions in particular, and to suggest any ways in which you might improve either. Revise your article accordingly.
- Proofread your final draft for errors in spelling, grammar, punctuation, and capitalization. Make a final copy and save it in your writing portfolio.

Main Idea and Supporting Details

"Houston, We've Had A Problem"

Excerpt from *Apollo 13: Space Emergency* by Michael D. Cole

INTRODUCTION

BUILDING BACKGROUND

On the morning of April 14, 1970, terrible news flashed across the country and around the world. An *Apollo* spacecraft on its way to the moon had suffered a serious accident. An oxygen tank had exploded, leaving the three-man crew dangerously low on electrical power and short on air to breathe. The astronauts onboard were in danger of being stranded in space. For the next three days, the world held its breath as the crippled craft circled the moon and headed back toward Earth. Would the ship make it? Could it land safely?

"Houston, We've Had a Problem" tells the story of the danger-filled flight of *Apollo 13*. As you read this excerpt, keep in mind that the *Apollo 13* spacecraft was made up of three attached but separate sections. The three astronauts traveled to the moon inside one section called the command module, which was named *Odyssey*. The command module was powered by rockets in the service module. The service module also contained other equipment, such as the oxygen tanks and fuel cells. Had things gone according to plan, with the crew to reach orbit around the moon, two of the astronauts would have entered the lunar module

Their relief at being safely back on Earth shows in the faces of *Apollo 13* astronauts (from left) Fred Haise, James Lovell, and John Swigert as they leave the rescue helicopter. The crew's April 1970 mission was supposed to be a routine trip to the moon, but it turned out to be anything but that.

85

Aquarius and landed on the moon's surface using the lunar module's own small rockets.

Had the surface mission been completed successfully, the astronauts would have flown back and reconnected with the command module, *Odyssey*. They would have climbed back into *Odyssey* and set *Aquarius* adrift into space.

Eventually *Aquarius* would have crashed back onto the moon. The rockets in the service module would have fired to carry the astronauts back toward Earth. When the ship arrived in Earth's orbit, *Odyssey* would have separated from the service module. *Odyssey* then would have carried the astronauts back to a soft landing at sea. Unfortunately, things didn't turn out that way. The excerpt you are about to read details what actually happened.

ABOUT THE AUTHOR

Michael D. Cole has been interested in space and the U.S. space program all his life. When he was a child, he dreamed of becoming an astronaut. Since becoming a professional writer, Cole has written several books about space exploration, including ones about *Vostok 1* and *Friendship 7*—the first Russian and the first American manned flights into space, the first moon landing by *Apollo 11*, and the building and launching of the *Columbia* space shuttle. Cole also has written biographies of astronaut and senator John Glenn, former President John F. Kennedy, and President Bill Clinton, as well as a book about Walt Disney and Mickey Mouse.

ABOUT THE LESSONS

The lessons that follow "Houston, We've Had a Problem" focus on main idea and supporting details. Using this excerpt as a model, you will see how author Cole builds a framework of main ideas and details to tell the story of the dangerous voyage of *Apollo 13*.

WRITING: DEVELOPING A DEBRIEFING REPORT

At the end of every space mission, NASA (the National Aeronautics and Space Administration) "debriefs" or interrogates, each astronaut. During the debriefing, each astronaut gives his or her personal account of everything that happened on the mission. At the end of this unit, you will write a debriefing report for one of the three *Apollo 13* astronauts. The following suggestions will help you begin thinking about your report:

- As you read "Houston, We've Had a Problem" decide which astronaut's debriefing report you would like to write—James Lovell's, John Swigert's, or Fred Haise's.
- Also as you read, try to imagine the thoughts and feelings of your chosen astronaut in various situations. Then jot down notes about the thoughts and feelings that you might have had in the same situations.
- Save your notes. You will use them later in this unit.

AS YOU READ

As you read this excerpt from *Apollo 13: Space Emergency*, ask yourself the following questions. They will help you focus on the main idea and supporting details that the author presents.

- What main idea is the author making about the *Apollo 13* mission?
- What details does the author use to support this main idea?
- How has the author organized this excerpt to show how his main idea and details connect with one another?

"Houston, We've Had A Problem"

Excerpt from *Apollo 13: Space Emergency* by Michael D. Cole

Many people believe that the number thirteen is an unlucky number. But the U.S. space program did not depend on luck.

American astronauts had already landed on the moon with *Apollo 11* and *Apollo 12*. Those missions had been successful because of hard work and long months of training, not luck.

So NASA (National Aeronautics and Space Administration) ignored superstition. They went ahead and named the next mission *Apollo 13*.

The mission began on April 11, 1970. *Apollo 13* lifted off at 2:13 P.M. from the launchpad at Cape Kennedy in Florida. It was an hour earlier at Mission Control in Houston, Texas. The controllers[1] in Houston watched *Apollo 13* leave the pad at 1:13 P.M. Houston time. On the military time clock it was 13:13 hours.

"Good luck. Head for the hills," said a controller to the crew of James A. Lovell, Jr., John L. Swigert, Jr., and Fred W Haise, Jr. The controller was talking about the crew's planned destination on the Moon. Lovell and Haise were

---

[1] people who control the flight and make final decisions when problems arise

supposed to land on the Moon in an area called the Fra Mauro uplands.

Fra Mauro was the site of a huge meteor crater near the Moon's equator. Scientists hoped the original impact[2] of the meteor millions of years ago had blasted samples of the Moon's inner bedrock[3] up to the surface. *Apollo 13*'s astronauts were going to collect samples of this bedrock so that scientists could learn more about the structure of the Moon.

Strange things started to happen just minutes after they launched the flight. One of the second-stage engines shut down more than two minutes early. The men in Houston corrected the problem. They fired the other four engines thirty-four seconds longer to make up for the lost thrust. Then the third-stage engine fired for nine extra seconds. *Apollo 13* entered Earth orbit in good shape, but they were forty-four seconds behind schedule.

The problems were corrected before the third-stage engine fired again. This "burn" sent *Apollo 13* out of Earth orbit and put it on course to arrive at the Moon in three days.

Hours later Jack Swigert—the command module[4] pilot— separated the command and service module (CSM) from the third-stage rocket. The command module was named *Odyssey* on this flight. Swigert turned the ship until it was facing back at the rocket. Next he moved in and docked[5] with the lunar module (LM). This module was housed inside the rocket assembly. The lunar module was named *Aquarius*.

Swigert then flipped a switch and *Aquarius* was separated from the rocket. *Odyssey* and *Aquarius*, now docked head to head, then continued toward the Moon.

---

[2] a very strong collision

[3] solid rock underneath the surface

[4] a self-contained spacecraft unit

[5] joined together

For the next two days the flight was very routine. The flight was so routine that the media[6] paid little attention to the mission. The TV networks no longer carried the live broadcasts that the astronauts made from space. Instead the broadcasts were taped, and small parts of them were shown later during the regular network news programs.

The three men had just finished one of their broadcasts when the mission suddenly turned frightening.

The date was April 13.

The crew was getting ready for an evening period of rest. Suddenly they heard a loud bang. A strong vibration shook the spacecraft.

Lovell was floating above his seat in the command module. He turned to look at Haise, who was floating in the tunnel that led to the lunar module hatch. Lovell thought Haise had made the sound by opening a valve in the lunar module. But Lovell saw the look of concern on Haise's face when the spacecraft shook. Haise had not opened any valve. The bang had been something else.

Swigert was in his couch in the command module. A master alarm was sounding in his headset. A yellow warning light on the instrument panel in front of him signalled a major loss of electrical power in the spacecraft. He slid across to the right couch and looked at the electrical system readouts. The voltage was dropping.

"Okay Houston, we've had a problem here," Swigert said. His words took the controllers in Houston by surprise.

"This is Houston, say again please."

"Houston, we've had a problem," Lovell said. He too was looking at the electrical readouts. "We've had a main B bus undervolt." This meant that the electrical power produced by one of the ship's three fuel cells was dropping. In fact, the fuel cell soon had no power at all.

---

[6] journalists and radio and television crews

"Roger. Main B undervolt," Houston said. "Okay, stand by *13*. We're looking at it."

More warning lights lit up on the display panel in the next three minutes. It soon appeared that fuel cells 1 and 3 were both dead. This situation automatically canceled the Moon landing mission. They could not make the trip on only one operating fuel cell. The astronauts were very disappointed.

Lovell continued to check all the systems aboard the spacecraft. The outlook grew worse. He was stunned when he noticed the quantity indicator light on oxygen tank 2. It read zero. Their situation was serious.

They were losing oxygen.

The oxygen was needed for several purposes aboard the spacecraft. But most important, the astronauts needed to *breathe*.

The oxygen in the tanks was also used to react[7] with hydrogen in the ship's fuel cells. The energy produced by this chemical reaction within the fuel cells provided all the electrical power in the spacecraft. Without proper quantities of oxygen, the fuel cells would not work. And if they did not work, electrical power in the spacecraft would fail.

There were three oxygen tanks aboard, but the level in oxygen tank 2 was now zero. There were only two oxygen tanks left to make power in the one remaining fuel cell.

A moment later Lovell looked at the quantity indicator light for oxygen tank 1. It too was dropping slowly as he watched it. He couldn't believe it.

Lovell was the mission commander. He was responsible for the lives of his crew. He watched the quantity level on oxygen tank 1 go down. Suddenly he realized that he and his crew might not make it home alive.

---

[7] to undergo a chemical reaction

No Turning Back

James Lovell was trying to figure out what had happened to *Apollo 13*. Two out of three fuel cells had shut down. One oxygen tank was empty. The level in another one was dropping. Only one good oxygen tank remained to operate the only remaining fuel cell.

They might soon be unable to generate any electrical power on the ship.

What had happened?

Lovell floated over to look out his window. He was not surprised to find a cloud of mist. "It looks to me that we are venting[8] something," Lovell said. "We are venting something out into space."

In Houston, chief flight director Gene Kranz tried to keep things under control. "Okay, let's everybody think of the kind of things we'd be venting," he said. No one could identify anything that would normally be venting. It was most likely the oxygen.

"Okay, now let's everybody keep cool," Kranz said. "We've got LM still attached, let's make sure we don't blow the whole mission."

Kranz was right about the lunar module. Whatever was wrong with the command module, it did not affect the attached lunar module. Kranz ordered the crew to power down the command module. This would conserve its power until they could learn exactly what was wrong. Even as they shut it down, *Odyssey* continued to lose power.

The astronauts were in a tough spot. But they did not have time to consider what a grim situation they were in. There was lots of work to do, so they simply got to it. Worrying or panicking would not make their situation better. And their situation was definitely not good.

It became clear to the crew and the people in Houston that there had been an explosion aboard *Odyssey*. The

---

[8] losing or letting out

explosion had ruptured oxygen tank 2 and was causing a slow leak in tank 1. The explosion had also damaged two of the three fuel cells.

In other words, the command module was crippled. The lunar module would have to become the astronauts' lifeboat.

The lunar module was designed to support two men for two days. Now it would have to support three men for four days. *Apollo 13* was 45,000 miles away from the Moon. They were five times that distance from Earth.

There could be no turning back. They could not generate enough power to make a direct return to Earth. They would have to make the trip around the Moon.

During the swing around the Moon, the LM's landing engine would fire and set *Apollo 13* on a trajectory[9] back toward Earth. The lunar module's engine had never been used for that before.

There was one other problem. The lunar module had no heatshield. It could not enter Earth's atmosphere. Only the command module with its heatshield was designed to reenter.

Lovell, Swigert, and Haise hung their hopes on two things. The first was that the lunar module could make the engine burn on the other side of the Moon and keep them alive until they could return to Earth. The second was that when they arrived at Earth, the command module would still have enough power to make a safe reentry. But their chances didn't look good.

The next morning the world woke up to the crisis aboard *Apollo 13*. People had not known much about the mission up until then. But by evening, people around the world were well aware of the dangers the astronauts faced.

Newspapers, radio, and television brought news and updates about the crippled mission. Soon millions of people

---

[9] a flight path

everywhere were familiar with the names of James Lovell, Jack Swigert, and Fred Haise.

Lovell and Haise were now in the lunar module *Aquarius*. Swigert stayed in the command module *Odyssey*. At the same time as Swigert was shutting down the command module, Lovell and Haise powered up *Aquarius*. Swigert used as little power as possible in *Odyssey*. He used only the cabin lights, the radio, and the heaters that would keep the reentry guidance systems ready at the end of the mission. Swigert later joined Lovell and Haise in *Aquarius*.

Engineers and technicians who had worked on the Apollo spacecrafts began to gather in Houston. They worked on new plans to help bring the crew home. A whole new return trajectory plan would have to be calculated and tested.

Other astronauts spent hours in the spacecraft simulators. They tested the engine burns and maneuvers[10] the crew would be using to get home. The plans seemed to work in the simulators. Everyone hoped they would work in space.

Apollo 13 neared the Moon. Fred Haise took a turn at sleeping in the darkened command module. They had been in space for sixty-nine hours. When Haise awoke, Lovell and Swigert took their turn to sleep. While they slept, some major decisions were being made in Houston.

The engine burn to bring the astronauts home would be made in several hours. There were disagreements on how to do it. Some people at Houston wanted to make a superfast burn that would get the astronauts home almost two days earlier. To do this, the service module part of the command module would have to be discarded. Only the crew capsule of the command module would be left. This would reduce the weight of the two ships by 50 percent.

---

[10] procedures or methods

There was a problem with this plan. If they discarded the service module, the capsule's heatshield surface would be exposed to space temperatures for forty hours. No one knew what this would do to the heatshield. It was too risky. No matter when the astronauts returned, a damaged heatshield would mean certain death.

NASA decided to keep the service module attached and make a burn that would bring the crew home in about four days. But would there be enough power to last the entire trip? Would the crew have enough water and oxygen to keep them alive and alert by the time they reentered Earth's atmosphere?

Teams in Houston worked on answering these questions. They worked out schedules for conserving power on the two ships. They worked out a plan for oxygen consumption. Engineers also devised a way that water could be transferred from the backpacks the astronauts would have used on the Moon. The astronauts also tried to build a device that would keep carbon dioxide from building up in the command module.

Many of the problems were being solved. It began to look as if a four-day return trip in the lunar module would work. Power for the ships, and oxygen and water for the crew should last that long. As long as nothing else went wrong.

Lovell got only a short nap in *Odyssey*. The spacecraft was dark and only minimum lighting was on in the lunar module. *Odyssey* was also becoming cooler. The cold and darkness of the command module gave the three men an eerie feeling. One of their spacecrafts was practically dead. And they were still so far from home.

By now the Moon dominated[11] the view out their windows. It no longer looked like a disk to the three men. They could now see the craters, hills, and mountains of the Moon below them. They got out cameras and took as

---

[11] overshadowed; controlled

many pictures as they could. But then there was plenty of work to do.

All the systems aboard the lunar module had to be charged up for the engine burn. The burn would occur after *Apollo 13* had swung around the Moon and was headed back home.

After seventy-six hours and thirty-two minutes in space, *Apollo 13* went into the shadow of the Moon. About thirty minutes later, the two ships passed behind the Moon and lost contact with Earth. For the next twenty-five minutes the Moon blocked all communications between Houston and *Apollo 13*.

When it emerged once again, the three men were on their way home. Finally the distance between them and Earth was narrowing with each passing second. Now it was time for the engine burn.

Swigert crawled back into *Odyssey*. Haise, who was the lunar module pilot for the mission, stayed in *Aquarius* with Lovell. Lovell threw the switch to start the burn. He and Haise controlled the burn manually for almost five minutes. They felt themselves being pushed toward the floor of the lunar module. Because the engine burn made no sound, this was the only way they could tell the burn was working.

Then the burn was over. Mission Control now showed that *Apollo 13* would arrive at Earth ten hours earlier than it would on a regular return trip. The successful burn was a boost to the astronauts' morale.[12] It looked as if they might make it.

Now there was a new concern to the people at Mission Control. The information they were receiving from the tracking stations was not good.

As *Apollo 13* returned toward Earth, something was pushing it further and further off course. If the drift continued, they would completely miss Earth.

---

[12] spirits; confidence

A Cold, Dark Journey

Mission Control realized that there must still be oxygen escaping from the spacecraft. This escaping gas was causing enough thrust to push *Apollo 13* off course. Engineers began calculating a course correction that would have to be made later.

It took the astronauts some time to power down the lunar module again. It had used a lot of power during the burn. Its power usage needed to get back down to a lower level if it was going to last the trip home.

By the time the power-down was completed, the three men were getting exhausted. It was about 10:30 P.M. Houston time on April 14. A full day had passed since the crisis began. None of the astronauts had gotten much sleep in the last two days.

Swigert was still too worried to sleep. He would be the command module pilot through reentry. He was worried about what *Odyssey*'s power level would be at reentry time. He asked Houston if they thought it would still have enough power when they returned to Earth.

"You think main bus B is good, don't you?" Swigert asked.

"That's affirm," the controller said from Houston. "We think it is, but we want to check it out anyway. We think you guys are in great shape all the way around. Why don't you quit worrying and go to sleep?"

Swigert thought that was easier said than done. But he knew they were right. Worrying would get him nowhere.

"Well," he said, "I think we might just do that. Or part of us will."

Swigert and Lovell went into the dark command module to get some sleep. Swigert took his orders to heart and was soon resting. But *Odyssey* was now much colder. Lovell found it impossible to sleep.

In the lunar module, Fred Haise talked to the capsule communicator (capcom), Jack Lousma. "From the sounds of all the work that is going on . . . this flight is probably a lot bigger test for the system on the ground than up here," Haise said.

"Yeah," Lousma replied, "we've been working it out a little bit."

"You guys have really got a tough job right now."

"Well everybody down here is 100 percent optimistic,"[13] Lousma assured Haise. "Looks like we're on the top side of the whole thing now."

After three hours, Lovell gave up trying to sleep. He returned to the lunar module and relieved Haise. "This is Lovell here," he said.

Jack Lousma was surprised. "Gee whiz," he said, "you got up kind of early didn't you?"

"It's cold back there in the command module," Lovell explained. The temperature in the command module was about 50° F. And it would get colder. There were two and a half days to go before splashdown.

Lousma suggested they might want to put on their spacesuits to guard against the falling temperatures in the ships. Lovell said no. He thought the bulky suits would make it too difficult to move around.

There were blankets in the emergency landing pack aboard the command module. But they were buried beneath a mound of other equipment. They didn't have the time or energy to dig for them.

The hours rolled by. Swigert joined Lovell in *Aquarius*, so Haise could get some rest. Lovell and Lousma discussed the upcoming course correction. The engine burn would be made in about ten hours.

They still had a long way to go. They could not stop whatever was venting from the spacecraft. And they had not entirely solved the problem of carbon dioxide buildup in the cabin. Lovell and Swigert tried to adapt one of the command module's odor canisters for that purpose.

---

[13] sure of good luck; hopeful

They used the canister to construct a box. This "mail-box" would filter the carbon dioxide from the air by sucking it through a hose taped to the canister. It was a pretty creative rig, but it looked like it might work.

James Lovell tried to put on a brave face as he worked. He got out a tape and played some music.

Capcom Lousma asked, "You got a Chinese band going up there?"

"Oh, sorry," Lovell said, "I forgot I was on mike."

"Sounds pretty good," Lousma added. The people in Houston were glad to hear the astronauts were keeping their chins up.

It was now April 15. Lovell, Swigert, and Haise had been in space for four days. They would be home in two days—if all went well.

Apollo 13 was now speeding up as Earth's gravity began to pull on the two ships. This too was a morale booster to the astronauts. But the next forty-eight hours would be the toughest for the crew. The power would remain very low and the cabin temperature would get much colder.

They needed to conserve[14] as much power as possible so they could give a good electrical charge to the reentry battery. This battery would power the command module through reentry. Without a good charge on the battery, Swigert would not be able to control the command module during reentry.

By evening the astronauts were powering up the lunar module for the course correction burn. It took more than an hour to set all the switches in the correct positions for the burn. At 10:30 P.M. Houston time, the lunar module engine fired. It was a difficult procedure.

Swigert watched the time clock. He told Haise when to press the buttons to start and stop the engine. Lovell had his eyes on a telescope. During the burn, he kept the tele-

---

[14] to save

scope's crosshair on the center of the crescent Earth ahead of him. At the same time he manually fired thrusters to keep it pointed on course. The burn was over in fifteen seconds.

Apollo 13 was now back on course for a splashdown in the Pacific in about forty hours. The lunar module was powered down again, and the astronauts settled in for some rest. They did not rest well in the growing cold. The temperature in the command module had fallen to about 44° F.

Early on the morning of April 16, Swigert began to switch electrical power from *Aquarius* to the reentry battery in *Odyssey*. It would take fifteen hours to charge the battery. But the power-down procedure in the lunar module had been very successful. It appeared there would be plenty of reserve to charge *Odyssey*'s battery up to full power for reentry.

Now the crew simply needed to last the remaining hours. The command module grew colder and colder. Water droplets were forming on the windows and the instrument panels. Because they had also been conserving their drinking water, Haise had become ill with a kidney infection and could not control his shivering. All three of them had consumed dangerously little water in the last two days. Houston was concerned that the lack of water would affect the astronauts' judgment and reactions during reentry.

The three men were fighting cold, hunger, thirst, and exhaustion. They had overcome some huge problems to get this far toward home. It looked like they might make it, if they could just hang on a little longer.

Hanging On

The last twenty-four hours were extremely tough on Lovell, Swigert, and Haise. The explosion had damaged the command module water tank. They had to ration their drinking water. The three men could drink only six ounces of water a day. That was less than one-fifth the normal requirement to keep them in good health. The doctors in Houston hoped the astronauts could still function as dehydration[15] set in.

As the temperature kept falling in the command module, water droplets continued to collect on the walls, windows, and control panels. They worried that the water might collect behind some of the instruments and cause a short-circuit in the controls. Or worse.

If the temperature continued to fall, the controls could freeze up. It was only about 38° F in the command module, just a few degrees above freezing.

The cold made the crew's life difficult. Lovell described how his crewmates were sleeping. "It's sort of humorous," he said. "Fred's sleeping place now is in the tunnel, upside down, with his head resting on the ascent engine cover. Jack is on the floor of the lunar module with a restraint harness wrapped around his arm to keep him down there."

Neither man tried to sleep in the command module because of the cold. The capcom for the next shift, Vance Brand, asked Haise about the cold.

"It's kind of a cold winter day up there, isn't it?" he said. "Is it snowing in the command module yet?"

"No, not quite," Haise replied. "The windows are in pretty bad shape . . . every window in the command module is covered with water droplets. It's going to take a lot of scrubbing to get that cleared off."

By evening in Houston, the instrument checklist for reentry was almost ready. They told Swigert he would need plenty of paper to write it down. But there were delays in getting the checklist relayed to the crew. Lovell sharply reminded Mission Control that there was no time for such delays.

"We just can't wait around here to read the procedures all the time up to the burn!" he said. "We've got to get them up here, look at them, and then we've got to sleep!"

---

[15] a condition caused by a loss of water in the body

Finally it was ready. It took two hours to go through the checklist.

Now everything was done. The astronauts could only wait as *Apollo 13* drew closer to Earth. The command module was getting colder by the minute. Lousma again talked to the crew.

"Wish we could figure out a way to get a hot cup of coffee up to you," Lousma said. "It would taste pretty good right now, wouldn't it?"

"Yes, it sure would," Lovell said. "You don't realize how cold this thing becomes . . . the sun is simply turning on the engine of the service module. It's not getting down to the spacecraft at all." Lovell meant that the command module was facing away from the sun, so that sunlight was falling only on the service module engine directly behind them. The rest of *Apollo 13* was in shadow. If the sun had been shining along the length of the two ships, both spacecrafts would have been much warmer.

"Hang in there. It won't be long," Lousma said.

It was now 3:00 A.M. on the morning of April 17. *Apollo 13* was set to splash down at about noon. Houston now decided there was enough power left to bring the lunar module up to full power. Two hours later the temperature in *Aquarius* had risen enough to take the chill off the crew.

Swigert later floated into the command module. It had also grown a little warmer in there. "Hey, it's warmed up here now. It s almost comfortable . . . I'm looking out the window now and that Earth is whistling in like a high-speed freight train."

The command module was finally powered up. To Swigert's relief, the controls and thrusters seemed to be working perfectly. It looked like there would be plenty of power to make the reentry.

The crew now got into position to jettison the damaged service module. The module's failure had almost cost them their lives. Now it separated and drifted slowly away. All three astronauts moved toward windows to get pictures of it. They could not believe what they saw. Lovell spoke first.

"And there's one whole side of that spacecraft missing!" he said.

"Is that right!" said the communicator in Houston.

"Right by the high-gain antenna, the whole panel is blown out, almost from the base to the engine." The side of the service module was a mess. The explosion had been a big one. As the astronauts looked at the wrecked service module, it was hard to believe they had been able to limp back from the Moon.

Apollo 13 was now only about 20,000 miles from Earth. They were almost home. The three men moved into the command module, which was now fully powered up. They closed the hatches between the two ships for the last time. With the flip of a switch they set *Aquarius* free. The lunar module had served them well. It had helped save their lives.

"Farewell, *Aquarius*. And we thank you," Mission Control said.

"She was a good ship," Lovell added.

The crew was now on a proper trajectory for reentry. Everyone hoped that the battery and the ship were ready to function. Whether they survived or not, the three astronauts knew their friends in Houston had done everything possible to get them home. As reentry began, Swigert thanked them.

"I know that all of us here want to thank all you guys down there for the very fine job you did," Swigert said. Capsule communicator Joe Kerwin talked Swigert smoothly through the reentry maneuvers. Swigert appreciated Kerwin's calm voice. "You have a good bedside manner, Joe."

"That's the nicest thing anybody has ever said," Kerwin replied.

Odyssey then slid into the Earth's atmosphere. The heat

caused by reentry friction cut off communications between Houston and the spacecraft. People watching on television or listening on radio around the world waited for the astronauts' voices to emerge from the blackout.

Three minutes passed. The people at Mission Control started to worry. Swigert should have answered by now. Joe Kerwin asked *Apollo 13* to acknowledge again and again. Another thirty seconds passed.

"OK, Joe," came Swigert's voice finally. Soon the parachutes deployed.[16] Cameras on the recovery ship U.S.S. *Iwo Jima* got television pictures of the capsule and its three parachutes. People around the world watched happily as the capsule floated safely toward its splashdown in the Pacific.

Apollo 13 was home!

---

[16] spread out; extended

REVIEWING AND INTERPRETING

Record your answers to these questions in your personal literature notebook. Follow the directions for each part.

REVIEWING

Try to complete each of these sentences without looking back at the excerpt.

Recalling Facts

1. The *Apollo 13* command module was named
  a. *Aquarius.*
  b. *Odyssey.*
  c. *Fra Mauro.*
  d. *Capcom.*

Understanding Main Ideas

2. On the way to the Moon, an explosion aboard *Apollo 13* caused the ship to lose
  a. fuel.
  b. hydrogen.
  c. oxygen.
  d. water.

Identifying Sequence

3. Water droplets began to collect on the windows of the command module *Odyssey*
  a. soon after liftoff.
  b. before the oxygen tank exploded.
  c. as *Apollo 13* circled the Moon.
  d. during the trip back to Earth.

Finding Supporting Details

4. *Apollo 13*'s emergency return to Earth was very difficult because the
  a. astronauts were suffering from heat exhaustion.
  b. spacecraft had lost too much fuel to make the trip.
  c. lunar module was designed for two men for two days.
  d. Earth and the Moon were moving away from each other.

Getting Meaning from Context

5. In the sentence "The explosion had ruptured oxygen tank 2 and was causing a slow leak in tank 1," the word *ruptured* means
a. turned.
b. split.
c. shrunk.
d. sealed.

INTERPRETING   To complete these sentences, you may look back at the excerpt if you'd like.

Making Inferences

6. If there was no power in the command module when the spacecraft reached Earth,
a. the astronauts would be forced to land in the lunar module.
b. the fuel cell would have to be recharged.
c. the command module would be abandoned.
d. the astronauts would not be able to land.

Generalizing

7. Astronauts Lovell, Swigert, and Haise
a. had trained for an emergency such as this.
b. remained calm and resourceful under pressure.
c. never realized how much danger they were in.
d. were in little danger after they successfully circled the Moon.

Recognizing Fact and Opinion

8. The following sentence states an opinion:
a. The lunar module would have to become the astronauts' lifeboat.
b. The spacecraft was dark, and only minimum lighting was on in the lunar module.
c. The last twenty-four hours were extremely tough on Lovell, Swigert, and Haise.
d. Houston was concerned that the lack of water would affect the astronauts' judgment and reactions during reentry.

Identifying Cause and Effect

9. Oxygen escaping from the ruptured tank
   a. pushed the spacecraft off course.
   b. collected in water droplets on the windows.
   c. cooled the interior of the ship.
   d. damaged the lunar module's rockets.

Drawing Conclusions

10. The following statement most accurately describes the flight of *Apollo 13*:
   a. NASA never should have used the unlucky number 13.
   b. The spacecraft was built from defective parts that caused the explosion.
   c. The oxygen tank was hit by a meteor.
   d. The astronauts and ground controllers worked together to bring the ship back safely.

Now check your answers with your teacher. Study the questions you answered incorrectly. What skills are they checking? Talk to your teacher about ways to work on those skills.

Main Ideas and Supporting Details

Writers of nonfiction begin with a topic, or subject, that they want to write about. In the selection you just read, the topic was the near-catastrophic flight of *Apollo 13*. To develop their topics, writers use a series of main ideas. Each paragraph expresses one main idea. The main idea tells what that paragraph is about. The writer then develops and explains the main idea of each paragraph through a series of supporting details. These details can include facts, opinions, examples, and evidence.

In this unit you will study the main ideas and supporting details in "Houston, We've Had a Problem," and you will learn to recognize the following:

1. **Topic and Main Ideas**   A writer's topic is the central point or idea that he or she wishes to present. What the writer has to say about the topic is usually divided into several main ideas, each of which is discussed separately.

2. **Supporting Details**   Each paragraph or series of paragraphs in narrative and expository nonfiction contains a main idea that is supported by details that further explain, clarify, or examine the main idea.

3. **Organization**   Writers give structure to their nonfiction by organizing their ideas and supporting details using several methods. Two common methods of organization are chronological (or time) order and cause and effect.

LESSON 1   TOPIC AND MAIN IDEAS

The topic of a piece of nonfiction is the central idea that holds the piece together. If a writer does not build the piece around a single, clear topic, the selection will be unorganized and difficult to understand. It will be just a collection of facts and details without a clear purpose.

To establish a clear purpose and provide direction, a writer uses a series of main ideas. Working together, the topic and main ideas form the framework for a piece of writing. Sometimes a main idea is expressed in a single sentence, which may be found at the beginning, the middle, or the end of a paragraph. At other times, a writer may use several paragraphs to develop one main idea completely. The main ideas in "Houston, We've Had a Problem" often appear as single sentences within a paragraph. Read the following paragraph from the selection. Can you tell which sentence contains the main idea of the paragraph?

> Strange things started to happen just minutes after they launched the flight. One of the second-stage engines shut down more than two minutes early. The men in Houston corrected the problem. They fired the other four engines thirty-four seconds longer to make up for the lost thrust. Then the third-stage engine fired for nine extra seconds. *Apollo 13* entered Earth orbit in good shape, but they were forty-four seconds behind schedule.

The first sentence of the paragraph states the main idea. It tells what the paragraph is about: the strange things that happened after the launch. The sentences that follow give details that explain what those strange things were.

EXERCISE 1

Read the following paragraph from the excerpt. Then use what you have learned in this lesson to answer the questions that follow it.

For the next two days the flight was very routine. The flight was so routine that the media paid little attention to the mission. The TV networks no longer carried the live broadcasts that the astronauts made from space. Instead the broadcasts were taped, and small parts of them were shown later during the regular network news programs.

1. What is the main idea of this paragraph? Explain why it is the main idea.

2. Is the main idea stated in a sentence, or is it implied, or given indirectly?

Now check your answers with your teacher. Review this part of the lesson if you don't understand why an answer was incorrect.

WRITING ON YOUR OWN 1

In this exercise you will use what you have learned to develop the main ideas that you will use in your debriefing report.

- Review your notes from the first writing exercise. Then ask yourself, "Had I been the astronaut I've chosen to write about, what would I have thought was the most important point to make to NASA officials about my experiences on *Apollo 13?*" Write down this central point; it will become the topic of your debriefing report.
- Make a list of three to five main ideas that support your topic. What do you think are the most important things to report to NASA scientists and engineers about your topic? Do you want to talk about the equipment? additional safety measures? emergency procedures? different training? Do

you have any comments about the assistance you received from Mission Control?

- Save your main ideas. Each of them will become the main idea of a paragraph or paragraphs in your debriefing report.

LESSON 2 | SUPPORTING DETAILS

As you learned in Lesson 1, the topic and main ideas of a piece of writing form its framework. Supporting details in each paragraph further develop the main idea and help complete the development of the topic.

When you are reading or writing, recognizing the details that support the main ideas is very important. Without details to support it, a main idea is often difficult to understand or accept. For example, imagine the response you'd get if you simply said to a parent, "I need a new bicycle." Without some supporting details for your idea, you probably wouldn't have much success. However, you might have more success if you said, "I need a new bike. My old bike has lost its brakes, and the frame is pretty rusty. I've grown six inches in the last year, and I need a bigger bike. My Boy Scout troop is taking a two-day bike hike next month, and a mountain bike sure would help on the rough terrain. And the bike I want is 50 percent off at the bike shop." The supporting details provide solid reasons why you need a new bike and might help convince your parent of your need for a new bike.

Writers use details to support their main ideas in several ways. In this lesson you will learn how writers use facts and examples to provide reasons, proof, or explanations to support their main ideas.

Facts Facts are statements that can be proved. In the following paragraph from the excerpt, the main idea is underlined. Notice that each of the other sentences supports the main idea. Each sentence contains facts that can be checked and proven.

> <u>The mission began on April 11, 1970.</u> *Apollo 13* lifted off at 2:13 P.M. from the launchpad at Cape Kennedy in Florida. It was an hour earlier at Mission Control in Houston, Texas. The controllers in Houston watched *Apollo 13* leave the pad at 1:13 P.M. Houston time. On the military time clock it was 13:13 hours.

Examples   Examples are supporting details that the writer gives to explain or illustrate a more general statement. Can you identify the general statement in the paragraph below?

> For the next two days the flight was very routine. The flight was so routine that the media paid little attention to the mission. The TV networks no longer carried the live broadcasts that the astronauts made from space. Instead the broadcasts were taped, and small parts of them were shown later during the regular network news programs.

The paragraph begins with a general statement of the main idea: *For the next two days the flight was very routine.* Each sentence that follows presents a specific example of how routine the flight was. Each sentence illustrates how little interest anyone had in the flight except the astronauts themselves and the people at NASA.

EXERCISE 2

Read this paragraph from the excerpt. Then use what you have learned in this lesson to answer the questions that follow it.

Teams in Houston worked on answering these questions. They worked out schedules for conserving power on the two ships. They worked out a plan for oxygen consumption. Engineers also devised a way that water could be transferred from the backpacks the astronauts would have used on the Moon. The astronauts also tried to build a device that would keep carbon dioxide from building up in the command module.

1. Find the sentence that states the main idea of this paragraph. Then list the details that support the main idea.

2. Explain how each of the details you listed supports the main idea.

Now check your answers with your teacher. Review this part of the lesson if you don't understand why an answer was incorrect.

 WRITING ON YOUR OWN   2

In this exercise you will use what you have learned in this lesson to develop supporting details for your debriefing report.

- Review your list of three to five main ideas, from Writing on Your Own 1.
- For each main idea, write down as many supporting details as possible. What facts support each main idea? Can you give an example of each main idea? Would a brief anecdote, or story, illustrate the main idea?
- For each main idea on your list, write a paragraph or several paragraphs using the supporting details that you have listed. Each of your main ideas should be expressed in a sentence somewhere in the paragraph or paragraphs.
- Save your work for the next writing exercise.

LESSON 3

ORGANIZING IDEAS

Clear connections are important in writing. A piece of nonfiction may have an interesting topic. It may have several informative main ideas and plenty of solid supporting details. However, it can still be confusing if the writer has not clearly organized the ideas. Without clear organization, it is difficult for readers to follow the writer's thoughts. As you learned in Unit 1, writers may organize information in chronological or spatial order, according to order of importance, by cause and effect, or by problem and solution. In "Houston, We've Had a Problem," Cole uses two methods of organization. He arranges the events of the *Apollo 13* mission chronologically, and within this chronology, he organizes information according to cause and effect relationships.

Chronological Order   When using chronological order, an author reports events in the order in which they occurred from first to last. In "Houston, We've Had a Problem" describing the events of the flight of Apollo 13 in the order in which they happened increases the suspense. The reader wonders throughout whether the astronauts will make it back to Earth and how they will solve each new problem that occurs.

To indicate the order in which events occurred, authors may state directly the time or date when something happens. At other times, they may use signal words and phrases, such as *meanwhile, later, soon after, before,* and *next,* to indicate when things happen. Look at the underlined words and phrases in the following paragraph. What clue does each provide about the order of events?

Apollo 13 neared the Moon. Fred Haise took a turn at sleeping in the darkened command module. They had been in space for <u>sixty-nine hours. When Haise</u>

<u>awoke</u>, Lovell and Swigert took their turn to sleep. <u>While they slept</u>, some major decisions were being made in Houston.

Cause-and-Effect Relationships   In every cause-and-effect relationship, one event brings about, or causes, the other. The event that happens first is the cause; the one that follows is the effect. Here is an example of a cause-and-effect relationship:

Because it began to rain on my walk to school, I arrived in the classroom all wet.

The rain is the cause; arriving wet is the effect. Writers often signal cause-and-effect relationships with words and phrases such as *because, next, therefore, since, so that,* and *in order that*. In the preceding example the word *Because* signals the cause.

Now look at the following passage from the selection. Can you recognize any causes and effects?

More warning lights lit up on the display panel in the next three minutes. It soon appeared that fuel cells 1 and 3 were both dead. This situation automatically canceled the Moon landing mission. They could not make the trip on only one operating fuel cell. The astronauts were very disappointed.

In this paragraph the dying of fuel cells 1 and 3 is the cause, and the lighting up of the warning lights is the effect. The fuel cells' dying also causes the moon landing mission to be canceled. In turn, the cancellation of the mission causes the astronauts' disappointment.

EXERCISE 3

Read this passage from the excerpt. Then use what you have learned in this lesson to answer the questions that follow it.

> *Apollo 13* was now speeding up as Earth's gravity began to pull on the two ships. This too was a morale booster to the astronauts. But the next forty-eight hours would be the toughest for the crew. The power would remain very low and the cabin temperature would get much colder.
>
> They needed to conserve as much power as possible so they could give a good electrical charge to the reentry battery. This battery would power the command module through reentry. Without a good charge on the battery, Swigert would not be able to control the command module during reentry.

1. Write the sentences in the first paragraph that describe cause-and-effect relationships. Underline each cause and enclose each effect in parentheses. Write any signal words in capital letters.

2. In the second paragraph, what effects of conserving power does the writer say will not occur until later? What effect will occur much sooner? What effects will be caused by not conserving enough power?

Now check your answers with your teacher. Review this part of the lesson if you don't understand why an answer was incorrect.

 WRITING ON YOUR OWN 3

In this exercise you will use what you have learned in this lesson to organize your debriefing report.

• Skim the selection and record everything that your chosen astronaut did during the flight of *Apollo 13.* What were his experiences and reactions? To help you organize the events that happened, make a chart such as the following one. Record when things happened to the astronaut and what events were occurring with the spacecraft at that time. The chart has been partially filled out as an example.

Astronaut: James Lovell		
Date/Time	**Event/Experience**	**Flight Record/Problems**
4/13 evening	• felt a strong vibration • looked at Haise	• first sign of trouble
4/13 evening	• checked all systems aboard the spacecraft	• master alarm is sounding • yellow electrical power warning light is flashing • fuel cells 1 and 3 are dead

• Assemble the paragraphs you wrote for Writing on Your Own 2. Then put them into the order that best matches the events you have recorded on your chart.
• Rewrite your paragraphs to include events from your chart. Use signal words and phrases to help readers follow the order of the time and sequence of the events.

DISCUSSION GUIDES

1. Imagine that the date is a recent anniversary of the famous *Apollo 13* mission and that the three astronauts are being interviewed on television. Form groups of four to play the roles of the astronauts and the interviewer. The student playing the interviewer should prepare a list of questions before the interview begins. The other three students should reread the excerpt and prepare answers to the interviewer's questions that they think the astronauts would have given. After a brief rehearsal conduct the interview in front of the class.

2. Space exploration is often dangerous. The U.S. space program has suffered eleven deaths over the years. In 1967 a flash fire burned up an *Apollo* spacecraft while it was being tested on the launchpad, and three astronauts were killed. In 1986 the space shuttle *Challenger* exploded shortly after takeoff, killing the entire crew, including the schoolteacher-astronaut Krista McAuliffe. As a class discuss how the dangers of space exploration compare with the dangers faced by land and sea explorers of earlier times. How do you think people would react today if the crew of a space shuttle or a space station were stranded and unable to return to Earth safely?

3. Do you know that there are several different types of astronauts? With a small group of classmates, research the different types and the qualifications that each type must meet. Share your findings in an oral report to the class.

4. Imagine that you were a ground controller in Houston for the *Apollo 13* mission. How do you think you would have felt as you tried to help the astronauts return safely? With a partner, write the dialogue for a conversation between the ground controller and one of the astronauts. Perform your dialogue for all or part of the class.

WRITE A DEBRIEFING REPORT

In this unit you have learned how nonfiction writers use main ideas and supporting details and how they organize them in their writing. Now you will use what you have learned to write a debriefing report.

Follow these steps to complete your report. If you have any questions about the writing process, refer to Using the Writing Process on page 217.

- Gather the following assignments that you wrote for this unit: 1) notes about the thoughts and feelings you might have had as an *Apollo 13* astronaut, 2) the topic of your debriefing report and three to five main ideas that support that topic, 3) several paragraphs containing details that support your main ideas, 4) a chart of events in chronological order and revised paragraphs based on the chart.
- Use these materials as the basis for your debriefing report to the engineers and scientists at NASA. As you write, remember that your readers already know a great deal about what happened from your radio reports and transmissions from space, but you were actually present and observed what happened. Try to tell your readers what you saw and thought, and describe things that they might not have learned about from your earlier reports.
- Be sure to use signal words and phrases in your writing to help your readers understand the chronological order of events.
- Ask a classmate to read your report and make suggestions for improvement. Then revise your report and share it with the class.
- Proofread your debriefing report for spelling, grammar, punctuation, and capitalization errors. Then make a final copy and save it in your writing portfolio.

I Got Myself a Start by Giving Myself a Start

Excerpt from *Madam C. J. Walker* by A'Lelia Perry Bundles

INTRODUCTION

BUILDING BACKGROUND

Madam C. J. Walker was a natural marketer. She introduced her hair products with free demonstrations, used her profits to build her business, and was her own best advertisement. Her products and her success transformed Madam Walker from a neat but shabby laundress with bad hair into a successful, fashionable businesswoman.

What do you think of when you think of inventors and inventions? Thomas Edison and the light bulb? Alexander Graham Bell and the telephone? These inventors became well-known figures because they developed new devices that changed the world forever. There are thousands of other inventors who, over the years, have created things that have improved our lives, but we don't know their names. Who, for example, invented the safety pin? the stoplight? super glue? the Post-it® note? The selection that follows is about one of these unknown inventors.

Madam C. J. Walker was the daughter of former slaves. Her parents were sharecroppers, and the family was very poor. Walker had little education and even less money, but she managed to overcome these obstacles by inventing and marketing hair-care products for African Americans. In a relatively short time, her products outsold the competition, and she built a large company that employed hundreds of people.

ABOUT THE AUTHOR

A'Lelia Perry Bundles is the great-great-granddaughter of Madam C. J. Walker. She is currently the Washington, D.C., producer of ABC television's nightly news show *World News Tonight*. Bundles was educated at Harvard University and the Columbia School of Journalism. She frequently gives speeches about the life of her famous great-great-grandmother.

ABOUT THE LESSONS

A biography is an account of a person's life written by someone else. An important goal of a biographer is to bring the subject of the biography to life for the reader. To do this, a biographer tries to reveal the character of the person he or she is writing about. The lessons that follow "I Got Myself a Start by Giving Myself a Start" focus on three methods biographers use to show readers the character of the people they are writing about—a physical description of the individual, an account of the person's actions, and the biographer's interpretation of the individual's character.

The selection you will read is one chapter from a biography of Madam C. J. Walker. As you read this chapter, notice how the author reveals Walker's character.

WRITING: DEVELOPING A BIOGRAPHICAL SKETCH

At the end of this unit you will write a biographical sketch (a short biography) of a person you know. The following suggestions will help you get started:

- Make a list of four or five friends, relatives, or neighbors who interest you and whom you admire. Think of people who have had an interesting or eventful life, or people who have been successful or have accomplished something you think is important. Has someone received an award? led an important group or organization? done something good for the community? Do you know someone who has done something brave? Do you know someone who has done a great deal for other people or for worthwhile charities?

- Write a few sentences about each person on your list, explaining why you think this person would make an interesting subject for others to read about.
- Save the list and sentences. You will need them for the next lesson.

AS YOU READ

Think about these questions as you read "I Got Myself a Start by Giving Myself a Start." They will help you understand how author Bundles reveals the character of Madam C. J. Walker.

- How does the author describe what Walker looked like? What pictures does she create in your mind? How does she describe changes in Walker's appearance?
- What actions by Walker give you clues to her personality and her attitude toward life?
- What does the author think of Walker? How can you tell?

I Got Myself a Start by Giving Myself a Start

Excerpt from *Madam C. J. Walker* by A'Lelia Perry Bundles

Sarah McWilliams watched her daughter skip off to school and smiled. Giving Lelia what she lacked herself—an education—made all her sacrifices seem worthwhile.

When the little girl disappeared from view, McWilliams walked through her St. Louis rooming house hallway to the backyard. There, clustered around the rickety porch, stood her wooden washtubs. Years later, she remembered the moment: "As I bent over the washboard and looked at my arms buried in the soapsuds, I said to myself, 'What are you going to do when you grow old and your back gets stiff?' This set me to thinking, but with all my thinking, I couldn't see how I, a poor washerwoman, was going to better my condition."

McWilliams looked at the baskets heaped with dirty clothes, then sighed and wiped her hands on her long, checkered apron. She raised an arm to her forehead, wiped the sweat with her sleeve, and pushed back her calico[1] bandanna. She knew her life was better than it had been when she left Vicksburg six years ago. Still, sometimes she could not help feeling discouraged.

---

[1] a coarse cloth having brightly colored designs

When she and her daughter arrived in St. Louis in 1888, McWilliams had headed for the city's black community. She found it filled with recently arrived people, many of them widowed mothers like herself. In this Mississippi River city of almost half a million residents lived one of the country's largest black populations, some 35,000 people. Swelled by migrants from the Deep South, the black community supported 3 weekly newspapers and more than 100 businesses.

St. Louis's pace was far swifter than Vicksburg's. Hurrying along its clamorous,[2] electric- and gas-lighted streets were white and black Missouri natives, transplanted easterners, and European immigrants. Dress styles ranged from ragged to elegant; vehicles included everything from expensive horse-drawn carriages to shabby peddlers' wagons. By the 1890s the city would claim the nation's largest brewery, its most important drug manufacturer, and its biggest tobacco factory.

Along the St. Louis riverfront, noisy, brightly lighted saloons and cafés attracted nightly crowds of gamblers and hustlers. . . . Ragtime, the infectious, syncopated[3] piano music that seemed to come from the heart of black St. Louis, poured from dance halls and bars. People tapped their feet to the rhythms of such popular tunes as "Ragtime Millionaire," with lyrics that captured the hopes and ironic humor of the community: "I'm afraid I may die of money disease / Don't bother a minute about what those white folks care / I'm a ragtime millionaire!"

McWilliams could not imagine herself a millionaire, but she had no trouble in finding work as a washerwoman. It was hard labor and carried no status, but it was better than working as a live-in servant, her only other option. Washing clothes at home meant she could keep an eye on Lelia.

---

[2] filled with loud noises

[3] marked by a musical rhythm that has offbeat or jazzlike accents

Taking pride in her work, McWilliams carefully scrubbed out spots, added just the right amount of starch, thoroughly cleaned the rust from her irons, and painstakingly pressed the delicate lace and ruffles of her customers' clothes. When she delivered her laundry, she walked with dignity, a basket of neatly folded clothes balanced atop her head.

McWilliams's delivery route often led her across the Eads Bridge, which spanned the Mississippi River and led to East St. Louis, Illinois. As she walked, she later remembered, she often marveled at the skill of the engineers who had built this great brick-and-steel structure. There must be a way, she had thought, to build a bridge to prosperity[4] for herself and Lelia. In her prayers, she asked God to show her the way.

McWilliams believed God would help her; she also knew she would have to help herself. Working long hours over her steaming tubs, scrimping on necessities, doing without luxuries, she managed to put aside a little money each week. By the time Lelia graduated from high school, her proud mother was able to send her to Knoxville College, a small black institution in Knoxville, Tennessee.

At about this time, McWilliams married again. Little is known of her second husband, John Davis; McWilliams rarely spoke of him except to remark that he was a heavy drinker. She apparently divorced him before her daughter went away to college.

Soon after her move to St. Louis, McWilliams had joined the St. Paul African Methodist Episcopal Church. Established in 1840, St. Paul was the first St. Louis church planned, built, and financed by blacks. Defying the pre-Civil War laws that forbade blacks to learn to read and write, St. Paul sponsored a secret school for its members, and it had long extended its aid to newcomers to the city,

---

[4] good fortune or financial success

helping them find houses and jobs, and supplying them with clothing and other necessities.

The women of the church had proved both friendly and generous to McWilliams. Deeply grateful, she vowed to help others in turn, although she had little money to contribute. After she settled into city life, she joined the Mite Missionary Society, the St. Paul organization that assisted needy members of the community.

Years later, a newspaper article described McWilliams's first activity for the society: "She read in the [St. Louis] *Post-Dispatch* . . . of an aged colored man with a blind sister and an invalid wife depending on him for support. Without acquaintance of any kind with the family, she went among friends in the behalf of the distressed people, succeeding in collecting $3.60 which she gave to them. . . . She felt it was her duty to do even more [so] she arranged for a pound party[5] through which means groceries in abundance were given, also a purse of $7.50."

Among the missionary society's members were a number of prominent, well-educated black women. Through them, McWilliams encountered a new world, peopled with prosperous, cultured blacks. She was dazzled by their stylish dress and formal manners and awed by their ability to organize themselves and become community leaders.

McWilliams was even more impressed by the black leaders who came to St. Louis for the 1904 World's Fair. Mingling with dazzled fairgoers were such luminaries[6] as poet Paul Laurence Dunbar, scholar and political activist W. E. B. Du Bois, and newspaper publisher T. Thomas Fortune. Even the great Booker T. Washington[7] was there, delivering two speeches to spellbound black audiences.

---

[5] a gathering for which each person donates a wrapped gift to be sold by auction; the proceeds are given to a charitable cause

[6] notable or famous people

[7] an American educator and black leader who was appointed the first president of Tuskegee Institute in Alabama

Also taking part in the festivities were 200 delegates of the National Association of Colored Women (NACW). After a meeting at St. Paul church, the NACW members proceeded to the fair, where they listened to an address by Margaret Murray Washington (the wife of Booker T.). Local newspapers ran Washington's picture and reported on her speech, marking the first time that the white St. Louis press had featured positive coverage of any black woman.

Gazing at the immaculately[8] groomed Margaret Washington, Sarah McWilliams reflected on her own appearance. Perhaps, she thought, if she improved it, she might gain some of the self-confidence exuded[9] by Washington and other successful black women. McWilliams always wore neat, crisply starched clothing, the better to advertise her skills as a laundress, but she was self-conscious about her hair; broken and patchy, it revealed her scalp in several places.

Countless black women shared McWilliams's hair problems. Sometimes inadequate diets, stress, and poor health caused hair loss; sometimes it was the result of lotions and treatments containing harmful chemicals. Advertisements for hair improvement products—Queen Pomade, La Creole Hair Restorer, Kinkilla, and Ford's Original Ozonized Ox Marrow, for example—crowded the pages of black newspapers.

The manufacturer of Thomas's Magic Hair Grower claimed its product would "cleanse the scalp of dandruff, stop it from falling, and make it grow even on bald spots." Because many blacks looked down on hair straightening as imitative of whites, Thomas's ads stressed that its product was "NOT A STRAIGHTENER." Although they disdained copying white females, few black women wore the traditional hairstyles and elaborate ornaments of their African foremothers, and many yearned for long hair.

---

[8] spotlessly; perfectly

[9] shown, demonstrated, given off

The "ideal" American woman of the 1890s had a full bosom, a tiny waist, and a great mass of hair, which she swept to the top of her head. Although not many women of any race could meet all these beauty standards, most tried for lengthy tresses.[10] Women whose hair refused to grow long wore wigs and hairpieces.

Sarah McWilliams asked God to keep her hair from falling out. She also tried a number of patented hair mixtures, including the Poro Company's Wonderful Hair Grower, but with little success. The St. Louis-based Poro Company hired local women to sell its products door to door; for a few months McWilliams worked as a sales agent when she was not washing clothes. Then she got a better idea: If she could devise[11] her own hair product, one that really worked for her, she could go into business for herself.

In early 1905 McWilliams informed friends that, with divine help, she had learned how to make the mixture she wanted. God, she later told a reporter, "answered my prayer, for one night I had a dream, and in that dream a big black man appeared to me and told me what to mix up for my hair. Some of the remedy was grown in Africa, but I sent for it, mixed it, put it on my scalp, and in a few weeks my hair was coming in faster than it had ever fallen out. I tried it on my friends; it helped them. I made up my mind I would begin to sell it."

Perhaps because she knew she would be in direct competition with the Poro Company, McWilliams decided to leave St. Louis before starting her new business. She had made one especially good friend in the city: Charles Joseph Walker, a sales agent for a local black newspaper. Except for Walker, she had little reason to remain in Missouri; she had divorced John Davis, and Lelia was still at school in Tennessee.

---

[10] a woman's long, flowing hair

[11] form; plan; or invent

Once again, McWilliams packed her belongings and headed for a new frontier, this one in Denver. Her brother had recently died, leaving his widow and four daughters in the Colorado city. McWilliams believed they could help each other. For the first time in her life, the 37-year-old woman would leave the Mississippi River area of her birth.

On July 21, 1905, McWilliams arrived at Denver's Union Depot with her savings: $1.50, about a week's pay for her work as a laundress. Colorado's mountains and wide blue skies astonished her, and she found Denver's crisp, dry air a welcome change from the steamy heat of St. Louis. Along the city's wide boulevards, cattlemen, silver miners, land speculators, and frontiersmen jockeyed for their share of the riches and adventure promised by the West.

Colorado's entire population was only slightly larger than that of St. Louis alone. When McWilliams arrived, fewer than 10,000 blacks lived in the state. Even here, where slavery had never taken root, they faced discrimination, but Colorado nevertheless offered blacks the chance to work in state and local government; many had started their own businesses.

Settling into the Mile High City, as Denver is known, McWilliams rented an attic room, joined the Shorter Chapel African Methodist Episcopal Church, and found a job as a cook. According to family records, her employer was probably E. L. Scholtz, a Canadian-born druggist who owned the largest, best-equipped pharmacy west of Chicago. His drugstore compounded both doctors' prescriptions and home medical remedies and tonics.

McWilliams probably consulted Scholtz about ingredients for the hair preparations she was concocting.[12] In any case, she spent her evenings working on her formulas and testing them on herself and her nieces. Finally, she came up with three products that met her requirements. She called

---

[12] preparing by mixing ingredients

them Wonderful Hair Grower, Glossine, and Vegetable Shampoo.

McWilliams saved her money carefully; before long, she could afford to leave her cook's job. To pay her rent, she took in laundry two days each week; the rest of the time she spent in mixing her products and selling them door to door. As a saleswoman, she usually wore a long, dark skirt and a white blouse; she carried her goods in a trim black case.

McWilliams soon proved herself a natural marketer, introducing her products with free demonstrations. After thoroughly washing a woman's hair with her Vegetable Shampoo, the saleswoman applied her Wonderful Hair Grower, a product that contained medication to combat dandruff and other conditions that sometimes caused hair loss. To complete the treatment, McWilliams applied a light oil to the customer's hair, then pressed it with a heated metal comb. This procedure softened the tight curls characterizing the hair of many people of African descent.

McWilliams had targeted her market well: Denver's black women began buying her wares with enthusiasm. At first, she used all her profits for raw materials and advertising. Her ads in the *Colorado Statesman*, a black newspaper published in Denver, generated mail orders, and her personal sales trips produced heartening results.

But McWilliams's best advertisement was herself. A customer who looked at a "before" picture, and then at the saleswoman herself, could hardly fail to be impressed. When McWilliams announced that her long, well-groomed hair was the product of her treatments, the customer was almost sure to place an order.

McWilliams, who had stayed in touch with her St. Louis friend, Charles Joseph Walker, wrote to him about her growing business. After providing a steady stream of advice by mail, Walker, known to all as C. J., showed up in Denver in person. Already fond of each other, the two soon decided to marry; their wedding ceremony took place on January 4, 1906.

Familiar with newspaper promotion campaigns, Walker helped his wife expand her mail-order business. Together, they manufactured and sold such products as C. J. Walker's Blood and Rheumatic Remedy and the newly named Madam C. J. Walker's Wonderful Hair Grower.

Sarah Walker began calling herself Madam not only to identify her marital status but to give her products more appeal. The title also evoked[13] thoughts of the world's fashion and beauty capital, France, where married women were called Madame. In the United States of the 1890s, women had few guaranteed legal rights; they could not vote, and in most states, could not even own property. Worse off, of course, were black women, who were frequently stereotyped[14] as childlike and ignorant. Thus, many black women in the public eye, such as opera singer Madame Lillian Evanti, adopted the title to convey an image of worth and dignity.

By the time the Walkers' business was bringing in $10 per week, C. J. Walker decided it had reached its full potential. Not so his wife: Sarah Walker believed that if they only knew about it, women all over the country would buy her Wonderful Hair Grower. Accordingly, she made plans for an extended sales trip.

Her husband and other advisers predicted she would not even earn enough to pay her expenses. She left anyway, setting out in September 1906 for what would become a year and a half of traveling to nine states, including Oklahoma, Louisiana, Mississippi, and New York. Within a few months she was making weekly sales of $35, more than twice the salary of the average white American male worker, and 20 times that of the average black woman worker.

---

[13] produced or created

[14] over-simplified; applying to an entire group; allowing for no individual judgments

By this time, Lelia, now 21 years old, had graduated from college. She moved to Denver to help run the mail-order business while her mother traveled. Elegantly dressed, nearly six feet tall, and regal of bearing, Lelia gave the company added distinction. She also demonstrated a flair for business, but even with the help of her four cousins, Anjetta, Thirsapen, Mattie, and Gladis, she could barely keep up with the orders her mother kept pouring in.

On the road, Sarah Walker was doing more than selling; she was training agents who could demonstrate and take orders for Walker products in return for a share of the profits. By the spring of 1908 she had signed on dozens of representatives and brought her company's monthly income to a breathtaking $400. Running a now vast mail-order operation, she decided to move her company closer to the nation's population centers.

After a visit to Pittsburgh, Walker selected the Pennsylvania city as her new base of operations. A thriving industrial and banking center, Pittsburgh boasted a sophisticated transportation system, a convenient source of steel for Walker's pressing combs, and a rapidly increasing black population.

In Pittsburgh, Walker rented an office on Wylie Avenue, the main street of the city's black community. She shared the bustling neighborhood with 45 churches, 5 lawyers, 22 doctors, and dozens of businesses, including tailor shops, restaurants, funeral parlors, and pharmacies. The area was home to a number of prosperous black families, but most of the city's blacks worked in service jobs or as laborers.

Although the bulk of Pittsburgh's mining and manufacturing jobs went to newly arrived European immigrants, waves of black southerners poured steadily into the city, eager to take whatever work they could find. Businesswoman Walker saw the influx[15] of blacks as a source of new agents and customers.

---

[15] inward flow

In the summer of 1908, Sarah Walker's daughter joined her in Pittsburgh. Together, the women opened a beauty parlor and a training school for Walker agents, which they called Lelia College. A graduate from the school would be known, they decided, as a hair culturist.

Word of the new college spread quickly. Applying for entrance were housekeepers, office cleaners, laundresses, and even schoolteachers, women whose needs and dreams Walker understood well. Over the next two years, Lelia College turned out scores of hair culturists, most of whom were delighted with their new careers.

In a letter to Walker, one graduate said, "You have opened up a trade for hundreds of colored women to make an honest and profitable living where they make as much in one week as a month's salary would bring from any other position that a colored woman can secure."

In 1910, the *Pennsylvania Negro Business Directory* ran a feature story about Walker, whom it called "one of the most successful businesswomen of the race in this community." Accompanying the article was a photograph of Walker, showing a woman dramatically changed in the course of only a few years. Posed with her hands clasped behind her back and her long hair pinned atop her head, Walker looked confident and dignified. Her high-necked, lace-bodiced gown more closely resembled her former customers' clothing than the threadbare gingham dresses she had worn during her days as a laundress.

As she rose in her career, Walker found herself sought out by the city's most prominent black citizens, including clergymen and the women who headed community and church organizations. The kind of people she had once admired from afar were now admiring her.

REVIEWING AND INTERPRETING

Record your answers to these questions in your personal literature notebook. Follow the directions for each part.

REVIEWING   Try to complete each of these sentences without looking back at the selection.

Recalling Facts

1. Sarah McWilliams's first job in St. Louis was as a
   a. servant.
   b. cook.
   c. washerwoman.
   d. drugstore clerk.

Understanding Main Ideas

2. As a young woman, Madam C. J. Walker was
   a. content with being a washerwoman.
   b. ambitious and wanted to succeed.
   c. envious of successful people.
   d. embarrassed by her parents' poverty.

Identifying Sequence

3. Sarah McWilliams changed her name to Madam C. J. Walker
   a. when she moved to St. Louis.
   b. before she moved to Denver.
   c. after she moved to Denver.
   d. when she opened Lelia College in Pittsburgh.

Finding Supporting Details

4. An example of Walker's good business sense was
   a. living in St. Louis.
   b. washing clothes for white customers.
   c. joining the National Association of Colored Women.
   d. moving to Pittsburgh.

*Getting Meaning
from Context*

5. "It was hard labor and carried no status, but it was better than working as a live-in servant, her only other option."
The word *option* means
a. choice.
b. training.
c. opinion.
d. offer.

INTERPRETING

To complete these items, you may look back at the selection if you'd like.

Making Inferences

6. Why was Lelia College such a success?
a. It was the first college for black women.
b. It gave many black women a chance to have a well-paying career.
c. Newly arrived immigrants were eager for an education.
d. It was the first college in Pittsburgh.

Generalizing

7. Which statement best describes the customers who used Walker's hair-care products?
a. They were mostly white women.
b. They were women who wanted to straighten their hair.
c. They were black women who wanted to improve their appearance.
d. They were unemployed housekeepers, office cleaners, laundresses, and even schoolteachers.

*Recognizing Fact
and Opinion*

8. Which of the following is a statement of opinion?
a. After a visit to Pittsburgh, Walker selected the Pennsylvania city as her new base of operations.
b. Sarah McWilliams's best advertisement was herself.
c. Among the missionary society's members were a number of prominent, well-educated black women.
d. Colorado's entire population was only slightly larger than that of St. Louis alone.

Identifying Cause and Effect

9. Walker moved to Pittsburgh because
    a. she wanted to be near her daughter.
    b. she was escaping racial discrimination.
    c. she could afford to live there.
    d. it was a good location for her growing business.

Drawing Conclusions

10. Which of the following is the best conclusion to draw about Walker?
    a. Her success was mostly brought about by her husband's business experience.
    b. Her success was mostly a result of luck.
    c. Her business became successful because she allowed others to share in its success.
    d. Once she became a success, Walker tried to hide her past.

Now check your answers with your teacher. Study the questions you answered incorrectly. What skills are they checking? Talk to your teacher about ways to work on those skills.

Biography

A *biography* is the story of a real person's life written by someone else. The person whose life story is being told is called the *subject*. Biographies are usually book length because they cover a subject's entire life.

Like all writers, biographers don't just *tell* us what the people they are writing about are like. They want to *show* the person's character. For example, a simple statement that Madeline is a kind person doesn't provide much information. Imagine, however, reading how Madeline adopted a stray dog with an injured leg and nursed it back to health. This is evidence that shows what Madeline is like.

A biographer carefully researches information to present a complete and accurate picture of his or her subject's life. Once a biographer has gathered all the facts and details of the subject's life, he or she must do more than simply list the information. The biographer forms an opinion about a subject's character and shares that interpretation with readers. An *interpretation* is one person's view of the meaning of certain words, events, or actions.

Biographers interpret facts by explaining their meaning and evaluating their importance. To help readers understand the subject's character or personality, the biographer sorts through the facts, deciding which are the most important and which support his or her opinion. He or she decides what events, people, or conditions influenced the subject's life. What were the turning points in the subject's life? By focusing on the answers to these questions, the biographer is able to provide a clear picture of the subject's life.

In this unit you will learn three ways that biographers reveal the character of their subjects:

1. **Physical Description**   Biographers give clues to their subject's character or personality by describing the person's physical appearance, how he or she dresses, and how he or she speaks.

2. **Actions**   Biographers also show what a person is like by describing the person's actions. The way a person acts often tells a great deal about what the person is really like.

3. **Author's Interpretation**   As biographers gather information about their subjects, they form thoughts and opinions about them. Does the biographer admire the subject? Does the biographer like this person? Does the biographer think the subject should have acted differently?

LESSON 1   PHYSICAL DESCRIPTION

Think about your friends and people you have recently met for the first time. Do you know someone who dresses very neatly, whose hair is always perfectly combed, and who never seems to get dirty or rumpled? What do these clues tell you about this person's character or personality?

Imagine two men sitting across the aisle from one another on an airplane. One man has very pale, smooth skin and a long, drooping black mustache. His head is shaved, and he wears an earring. There is a small tattoo of a musical note on his left cheek, and he has rings on all of his long, slender fingers. The other man has deeply tanned, leathery skin. His graying hair is cut short and combed flat. The man's hands are very large and calloused. There are deep wrinkles at the corners of his eyes. He is wearing a faded flannel shirt and well-worn jeans held up by a belt with a large silver buckle. On his feet are a pair of highly polished cowboy boots. As you look at these two men, you begin to form ideas about what they are like and where they come from.

Writers provide information about the people they write about in this same way. Describing a person's physical appearance is one way writers help us get to know and understand the subject in a biography.

Read this paragraph from the selection. As you read, notice how Bundles describes McWilliams. What clues does this description give you about the kind of person McWilliams is?

> Gazing at the immaculately groomed Margaret Washington, Sarah McWilliams reflected on her own appearance. Perhaps, she thought, if she improved it, she might gain some of the self-confidence exuded by Washington and other successful black women. McWilliams always wore neat, crisply starched clothing, the better to advertise her skills as a laundress, but she was self-conscious about her hair; broken and patchy, it revealed her scalp in several places.

The author is telling readers what McWilliams is thinking. McWilliams realizes that her appearance influences not only how other people act toward her but also how she feels about herself. By describing how McWilliams dresses, Bundles suggests that her great-great-grandmother is trying to create a better image of herself for others to see—an image that will fit the new role in life that she wants for herself. But McWilliams is self-conscious about her broken and patchy hair. From this, readers can tell that she has not yet gained the appearance she wants. It is also clear that McWilliams fears she can not measure up to the appearance or success of the African-American women she admires.

EXERCISE 1

Read these two passages from the selection. Use what you have learned in this lesson to answer the questions that follow them.

> McWilliams looked at the baskets heaped with dirty clothes, then sighed and wiped her hands on her long, checkered apron. She raised an arm to her forehead, wiped the sweat with her sleeve, and pushed back her

calico bandanna. She knew her life was better than it had been when she left Vicksburg six years ago. Still, sometimes she could not help feeling discouraged.

In 1910 the *Pennsylvania Negro Business Directory* ran a feature story about Walker, whom it called "one of the most successful businesswomen of the race in this community." Accompanying the article was a photograph of Walker, showing a woman dramatically changed in the course of only a few years. Posed with her hands clasped behind her back and her long hair pinned atop her head, Walker looked confident and dignified. Her high-necked, lace-bodiced gown more closely resembled her former customers' clothing than the threadbare gingham dresses she had worn during her days as a laundress.

1. Compare and contrast these two physical descriptions, one at an early period in McWilliams's life and the other several years later.

2. What do these two descriptions tell you about changes in the subject? How do you think she has changed? How do you think she has remained the same?

Now check your answers with your teacher. Review this lesson if you don't understand why an answer was incorrect.

 WRITING ON YOUR OWN 1

In this exercise use what you have learned in this lesson to write a physical description of the subject of your biographical sketch. Follow these steps:

- Reread the list of possible subjects you made for Developing a Biographical Sketch. Choose a person from your list to be the subject of your sketch.
- Copy the graphic organizer that follows onto a sheet of paper.

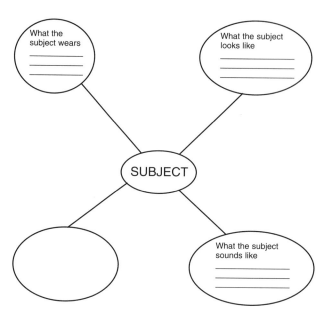

- Think about the person you've chosen as your subject. Use the graphic organizer to help you describe as many details as possible about this person. What does your subject *look* like? What color are his or her eyes and hair? Does the person have a pleasant smile? What about the rest of this person's appearance? Does he or she have long legs? Is this person thin? Describe the kind of clothing the subject wears. Does this person like a certain style or fashion? What does he or she *sound* like? Does the subject have a soft, clear voice or a loud, raspy one? Does this person have a large or unusual vocabulary? If you think of other categories for the organizer, add them.
- Using the details you have listed, write one or two paragraphs describing what the subject of your biography looks and sounds like.

LESSON 2 ACTIONS

Writers often describe a person's actions as a way of revealing character. A person's actions can tell you much about what the person believes and what his or her inner qualities or values are. In fact, as the old saying "Actions speak louder than words" suggests, a person's actions may show more than appearance or words can.

Imagine that you know a boy who always punches you in the shoulder when he meets you and always has a sarcastic remark to make when you speak to him. You will probably form a negative opinion of him. But imagine that one day you see him wheeling a woman in a wheelchair around the supermarket. He is smiling, joking, and helping her with her shopping. When you meet him in the aisle, he introduces you to his mother. After this experience your opinion of his character is likely to change. You realize that he has many responsibilities at home, and you can see that there is a kind, gentle side to him that is not apparent on the surface.

As you read this paragraph from the selection, what do you learn about McWilliams's character from her actions?

> Taking pride in her work, McWilliams carefully scrubbed out spots, added just the right amount of starch, thoroughly cleaned the rust from her irons, and painstakingly pressed the delicate lace and ruffles of her customers' clothes. When she delivered her laundry, she walked with dignity, a basket of neatly folded clothes balanced atop her head.

Bundles *tells* her readers directly that McWilliams takes pride in her work, but she *shows* exactly what this means: McWilliams carries out each step in cleaning her customers' clothes with great care. It is clear that she is an expert at what she does. She knows just what to do and how to do it. Finally, Bundles describes McWilliams's dignified walk when she delivers her laundry. All these actions reveal something about McWilliams's values. She takes pride in doing her job well.

EXERCISE 2

Read this passage from the selection. Use what you have learned in this lesson to answers the questions that follow it.

By the time the Walkers' business was bringing in $10 per week, C. J. Walker decided it had reached its full potential. Not so his wife: Sarah Walker believed that if they only knew about it, women all over the country would buy her Wonderful Hair Grower. Accordingly, she made plans for an extended sales trip.

Her husband and other advisers predicted she would not even earn enough to pay her expenses. She left anyway, setting out in September 1906 for what would become a year and a half of traveling to nine states, including Oklahoma, Louisiana, Mississippi, and New York. Within a few months she was making weekly sales of $35, more than twice the salary of the average white American male worker, and 20 times that of the average black woman worker. . . .

On the road, Sarah Walker was doing more than selling; she was training agents who could demonstrate and take orders for Walker products in return for a share of the profits. By the spring of 1908, she had signed on dozens of representatives and brought her company's monthly income to a breathtaking $400. Running a now vast mail-order operation, she decided to move her company closer to the nation's population centers.

1. What have you learned about Walker's character from her actions in this passage?

2. What did you learn about Walker's business abilities?

Now check your answers with your teacher. Review this lesson if you don't understand why an answer was incorrect.

WRITING ON YOUR OWN [2]

In this exercise you will use what you have learned in this lesson to describe an action by your subject. Follow these steps:

- Think about the person you have chosen as the subject of your biographical sketch. Is this person brave? clever? kind? a good athlete? Think of one action from your subject's life that reveals part of this person's character or personality.
- Write several paragraphs describing this action or event in your subject's life. Try to tell what happened in a way that *shows* the person's character, rather than telling your readers what it is. For example, suppose you are writing about your subject's brave act. Instead of using words such as *bravely* or *courageously*, explain how your subject acted in a situation that demonstrated his or her bravery.

LESSON 3   AUTHOR'S INTERPRETATION

So far, you have learned that biographers reveal their subjects' characters by presenting physical descriptions and showing how their subjects act in various situations. A biographer also presents his or her own thoughts and opinions about the subject.

As a biographer gathers information through research, he or she learns more and more about a subject. The writer sees how this person acts and reacts in different situations, and draws conclusions from these facts to form an opinion. To help readers understand the subject's character or personality, the biographer sorts through all the facts and decides which are the most important. He or she tells what events, people, or conditions had the greatest effect on the subject's life. The biographer describes the inner forces that caused the subject to act as he or she did. The biographer also decides what the turning points in the subject's life were. By doing all this, the biographer is interpreting the subject's life.

Read these two sentences from the beginning of the selection. In which sentence does Bundles give an interpretation of the facts?

> Sarah McWilliams watched her daughter skip off to school and smiled. Giving Lelia what she lacked herself—an education—made all her sacrifices seem worthwhile.

The first sentence describes what McWilliams did: she watched her daughter skip off to school, and she smiled. The second sentence is the writer's interpretation of why McWilliams smiled: she smiled because giving Lelia an education was worth all her sacrifices. If you saw a mother smiling as her daughter went off to school, you might think of a number of reasons for the smile. She might be glad to have the house to herself. Perhaps her daughter had been sick, and the mother was glad she was healthy again. Maybe the mother was smiling because the girl had just told her a joke. The possibilities are endless.

By giving a reason for McWilliams's smile, Bundles is providing her own interpretation. Bundles is showing that McWilliams cared deeply about her daughter and that she was making sacrifices in her own life so that her daughter would have a better life. It is obvious that the author respects and admires McWilliams.

EXERCISE 3

Read this passage from the selection. Use what you have learned in this lesson to answer the questions that follow it.

> McWilliams's delivery route often led her across the Eads Bridge, which spanned the Mississippi River and led to East St. Louis, Illinois. As she walked, she later remembered, she often marveled at the skill of the engi-

neers who had built this great brick-and-steel structure. There must be a way, she had thought, to build a bridge to prosperity for herself and Lelia. In her prayers, she asked God to show her the way.

McWilliams believed that God would help her; she also knew she would have to help herself. Working long hours over her steaming tubs, scrimping on necessities, doing without luxuries, she managed to put aside a little money each week. By the time Lelia graduated from high school, her proud mother was able to send her to Knoxville College, a small black institution in Knoxville, Tennessee.

1. Why do you think Bundles decided to include information, in the first paragraph, about Walker's delivery route and her thoughts as she crossed the bridge? How does this information reveal the author's attitude toward Walker?

2. What is Bundles telling you about her subject in that paragraph?

Now check your answers with your teacher. Review this part of the lesson if you don't understand why an answer was incorrect.

WRITING ON YOUR OWN 3

In this exercise you will use what you have learned in this lesson to add your own interpretation of your subject's character. Follow these steps:

- Reread the sentences you wrote for Developing a Biographical Sketch, explaining why you think the person you chose would make an interesting subject for your sketch.
- Write a paragraph expressing your opinion about your subject's character. Your interpretation should include details about things your subject has said or done that support your interpretation.

DISCUSSION GUIDES

1. The title of this selection, "I Got Myself a Start by Giving Myself a Start," comes from Walker's own description of how she started her business. In a small group discuss what Walker meant by her statement. What do you think contributed most to Walker's success—the quality of her hair products, her good business sense, or her hard work and determination? Or do you think all three contributed equally?

2. Imagine that you are Walker and are making plans for your first extended sales trip across the country. In a group of three write out a conversation among Walker, her husband, and her daughter, Lelia, as they consider how to make the trip profitable. Act out your dialogue for the class.

3. As a class discuss whether you think it is easier or more difficult today for a woman to start her own business and be successful than it was in Walker's time. Give reasons for your answer.

WRITE A BIOGRAPHICAL SKETCH

In this unit you have learned three ways that biographers reveal the character of their subjects. Now you will use what you have learned to write a biographical sketch of a person you know well.

Follow these steps to complete your biographical sketch. If you have any questions about the writing process, refer to Using the Writing Process on page 217.

- Gather and review the following pieces of writing you did for this unit: 1) the list of possible subjects with accompanying sentences, 2) the graphic organizer and paragraphs giving a physical description of your subject, 3) the paragraphs describing your subject's action, 4) the paragraphs expressing your opinion of your subject's character.
- Write an introductory paragraph for your biographical sketch. Introduce your subject to your readers and explain why they will be interested to know about this person.
- To the introductory paragraph, add the paragraphs giving a physical description of your subject, describing an action of your subject, and giving your opinion about your subject's character.
- Reread your sketch. Have you given an accurate and vivid physical description of your subject? Does the example of your subject in action clearly reveal his or her character? Add more details if you need them to support your interpretation of your subject.
- Exchange biographical sketches with a classmate. Critique each other's work and make suggestions for improvements. If any suggestions seem valid, revise your sketch accordingly.
- Proofread your final draft for errors in spelling, grammar, punctuation, and capitalization. Make a final copy and save it in your writing portfolio.

The Diary

A Child's Life in Sarajevo

Excerpts from *Zlata's Diary* by Zlata Filipović

INTRODUCTION

BUILDING
BACKGROUND

In 1984 the world was introduced to a beautiful city. The 1984 Winter Olympic Games were held in and around the city of Sarajevo in Yugoslavia. A lot has happened to Sarajevo since then, as you will find out when you read excerpts from the diary of an 11-year-old girl who lived there.

Sarajevo is in the Republic of Bosnia and Herzegovina (usually called Bosnia), which is located in the Balkan Peninsula. Bosnia is bordered on the north and west by Croatia and on the east and south by Serbia and Montenegro. The three major groups who live in Bosnia are Muslims, Serbians, and Croatian.

In March 1992 Bosnia declared its independence from Yugoslavia. That's when everyone's life changed forever. The Serbs wanted Bosnia to stay a part of Yugoslavia—a Serb-controlled country. Muslims and Croats wanted Bosnia to be independent. Soon civil war broke out among the Serbs, the Croats, and the Muslims. Fierce three-way fighting began around the capital, Sarajevo. Bosnian Serb forces surrounded the city. As a result of this fighting, much of the city was destroyed. Thousands of non-Serbs were

Before March 1992 Muslims, Serbs, and Croats lived peacefully togothor in Sarajovo, a beautiful, bustling city in the Republic of Bosnia and Herzegovina in Yugoslavia. Civil war broke out when Bosnia-Herzegovina declared its independence from Yugoslavia, and much of the city was destroyed in the fighting that followed.

killed or removed from the Bosnian area. Thousands of children were killed or wounded. It was estimated that by the end of 1994 more than two million people had been driven from their homes.

ABOUT THE AUTHOR

In 1991, just six months before Bosnia declared itself an independent country, an 11-year-old girl named Zlata Filipović began her diary. As you will see, Zlata led a very normal and happy life. She worked hard at school, practiced the piano, sang in the choir, played tennis, and loved to ski. Zlata and her friends spent holidays together, went to the movies, and had slumber parties.

Little did Zlata know when she began her diary how much her life and the lives of her parents and friends would change. Soon the electricity would be cut off. The phone would go dead. Then all the running water would stop. Worst of all, the food supplies would disappear. The family would have to wait in line for hours in the hope of getting a loaf of bread. But the wait was not the most dangerous part. Each day as they stood in line, they faced artillery shelling and gun shots from snipers. There was no water for bathing or to use in the toilets. To get their drinking water, they had to wait in another long line and face another risk of being shot.

Finally, in 1993 Zlata and her family were able to leave Sarajevo with the help of the French and the United Nations. On December 23 they left on a United Nations plane for Paris.

ABOUT THE LESSONS

The lessons that follow "A Child's Life In Sarajevo" focus on the facts, feelings, and thoughts in Zlata's diary and how her diary is a record of history.

Like most people who keep a diary, Zlata originally wrote for her own personal satisfaction. She recorded her feelings and thoughts about her life as well as the events that were making history. One way to appreciate a writer's diary is to examine its various elements. Do you get a sense of what it is like where she lives? Does she seem honest about her feelings? Does she express her thoughts clearly? What can you tell about Zlata's character? The lessons in this unit will help you understand the diary as a type of autobiographical nonfiction.

WRITING: DEVELOPING A DIARY ENTRY

At the end of this unit, you will write your own diary entry. The suggestions below will help you get started:

- Think about what has happened in your life in each of the past few days. Recall some particular events. They can be ordinary events—such as going to the movies with a close friend, having a test or quiz at school, or going to basketball practice—or they can be important events that were not so ordinary.
- Make a list of several of these events. Don't worry if you feel nothing important has happened to you recently. As you read the selection, you'll notice that when Zlata started her diary, she wrote about pretty routine happenings in her life.
- Next to each event write a sentence briefly describing the event.

AS YOU READ

Think about these questions as you read "A Child's Life in Sarajevo." They will help you identify and understand the elements of a diary.

- How is the setting important to Zlata's life?
- What is it like to be 11 years old in Sarajevo?
- What different emotions does Zlata express in her diary entries?
- What does Zlata look forward to? What are some of the things that Zlata is concerned about? What do her concerns tell you about her?

A Child's Life in Sarajevo

Excerpts from *Zlata's Diary* by Zlata Filipović

CAST OF CHARACTERS

Zlata's Family and Friends

Melica, her father's sister

Braco Bobar, her mother's brother

Bobar Family, close neighbors and family friends—**Auntie Boda** and **Uncle Zika,** the parents of **Maja** and **Bojana**

Braco and Keka Lajtner, friends—the parents of **Martina** and **Matea**

Mirna, Zlata's best friend

Neda, mother's best friend from work

Nedo, refugee—a friend and neighbor

Srdjan and **Bokica,** friends of Zlata's mother—the parents of **Andre** and **Vanja**

Janine, a journalist for the *London Sunday Times* newspaper

Alexandra, a member of a Canadian television crew

Monday, September 2, 1991

Behind me—a long, hot summer and the happy days of summer holidays; ahead of me—a new school year. I'm starting fifth grade. I'm looking forward to seeing my friends at school, to being together again. Some of them I haven't seen since the day the school bell rang, marking the end of term. I'm glad we'll be together again, and share all the worries and joys of going to school.

Mirna, Bojana, Marijana, Ivana, Maša, Azra, Minela, Nadža—we're all together again.

Sunday, October 6, 1991

I'm watching the American Top 20 on MTV. I don't remember a thing, who's in what place. I feel great because I've just eaten a "Four Seasons" **pizza** with ham, cheese, ketchup, and mushrooms. It was yummy. Daddy bought it for me at Galija's (the pizzeria around the corner). Maybe that's why I didn't remember who took what place—I was too busy enjoying my pizza.

I've finished studying and tomorrow I can go to school **bravely**, without being afraid of getting a bad grade. I deserve a good grade because I studied all weekend and I didn't even go out to play with my friends in the park. The weather is nice and we usually play "monkey in the middle," talk, and go for walks. Basically, we have fun.

[Zlata and her family go to their home in the country]

Sunday, October 13, 1991

It was wonderful in Crnotina. I like our house (it's really unusual) and the surrounding countryside more and more every time we go. We picked pears, apples, walnuts; we took pictures of a clever little squirrel that stole the walnuts; in the evening we had a barbecue—my specialty is ćevapčići [grilled meat rolls]. Grandma made apple strudel. I collected different leaves for the herbarium[1] and played with Ati.

Autumn has already replaced summer. Slowly but surely it is painting and coloring nature with its brush. The leaves are turning yellow, red, and they are falling. The days are

---

[1] a dried-plant collection

getting shorter and it's colder. Autumn is really nice too! In fact, every season's nice in its own way. Somehow I don't notice and don't feel the beauty of nature when I'm in town the way I do when I'm in Crnotina. In Crnotina it smells good, it caresses me, it calls me into its embrace.[2] I had a really nice rest enjoying and feeling the beauty of nature.

Saturday, October 19, 1991

Yesterday was a really awful day. We were ready to go to Jahorina (the most beautiful mountain in the world) for the weekend. But when I got home from school, I found my mother in tears and my father in uniform. I had a lump in my throat when Daddy said he had been called up by the police reserve. I hugged him, crying, and started begging him not to go, to stay at home. He said he had to go. Daddy went, and Mommy and I were left alone. Mommy cried and phoned friends and relatives. Everyone came immediately. . . . They all came to console us and to offer their help. Keka took me to spend the night with Martina and Matea. When I woke up in the morning, Keka told me everything was all right and that Daddy would be home in two days.

I'm home now; Melica is staying with us and it looks as though everything will be all right. Daddy should be home the day after tomorrow. Thank God!

Thursday, November 14, 1991

Daddy isn't going to the reserves anymore. Hooray!!! . . . Now we'll be able to go to Jahorina and Crnotina on weekends. But, gasoline has been a problem lately. Daddy often spends hours waiting in line for gasoline; he goes outside of town to get it and often comes home without getting the job done. . . .

---

[2] a hug

War in Croatia, war in Dubrovnik, some reservists[3] in Herzegovina. Mommy and Daddy keep watching the news on TV. They're worried. Mommy often cries looking at the terrible pictures on TV. They talk mostly politics with their friends. What is politics? I haven't got a clue. And I'm not really interested. I just finished watching *Midnight Caller* on TV.

Thursday, December 26, 1991

. . . It was Christmas yesterday. We went to M&M's (Martina and Matea's). It was wonderful. A big Christmas tree. Christmas presents and the proverbial[4] Christmas table. And Bokica was there with Andrej. And there was a surprise. Srdjan phoned. Everyone was happy and sad at the same time. There we were all warm, surrounded by Christmas decorations and presents, with lots of wonderful food and drink in front of us. And there he was, like everybody else in Dubrovnik . . . in a war. This war will pass, Srdjan, we'll all be together again! You've got to hold on!!! I'm keeping my fingers crossed for you and for all the people and children in Dubrovnik.

It'll be New Year's Eve soon. The atmosphere seems different than before. Mommy, Daddy, and our friends and family aren't planning a New Year's Eve party this year. They don't talk about it much. Is it because of the war in Dubrovnik? Is it some kind of fear? I don't know or understand a thing. . . .

Thursday, March 5, 1992

Oh, God! Things are heating up in Sarajevo. On Sunday (March 1), a small group of armed civilians (as they say on TV) killed a Serbian wedding guest and wounded the priest. On March 2 (Monday) the whole city was full of barricades. There were "1,000" barricades. We didn't even

---

[3] the soldiers in the military forces of a country who are not part of the regular army services

[4] expressed in a proverb; a short, old, wise saying; traditional

have bread. At 6:00 people got fed up and went out into the streets. The procession set out from the cathedral. It went past the parliament building and made its way through the entire city. Several people were wounded at the Marshal Tito army barracks. People sang and cried "Bosnia, Bosnia," "Sarajevo, Sarajevo," "We'll live together" and "Come outside." . . .

On March 4 (Wednesday) the barricades were removed, the "kids" [a popular term for politicians] had come to some agreement. Great?!

That day our art teacher brought in a picture for our class-mistress[5] (for March 8, Women's Day). We gave her the present, but she told us to go home. Something was wrong again! There was a panic. The girls started scream-ing and the boys quietly blinked their eyes. Daddy came home from work early that day too. But everything turned out OK. It's all too much!

Monday, March 30, 1992

Hey, Diary! You know what I think? Since Anne Frank[6] called her diary Kitty, maybe I could give you a name too. . . .

I'm thinking, thinking. . . .

I've decided! I'm going to call you MIMMY.

Thursday, April 9, 1992

Dear Mimmy,

I'm not going to school. All the schools in Sarajevo are closed. There's danger hiding in these hills above Sarajevo. But I think things are slowly calming down. The heavy shelling and explosions have stopped. There's occasional gunfire, but it quickly falls silent. Mommy and Daddy aren't going to work. They're buying food in huge quantities. Just in case, I guess. God forbid!

---

[5] head teacher

[6] a 13-year-old schoolgirl in Holland who wrote a famous diary while she and her family were in hiding from the Nazis

Still, it's very tense. Mommy is beside herself; Daddy tries to calm her down. Mommy has long conversations on the phone. She calls, other people call, the phone is in constant use.
Zlata

Saturday, May 2, 1992

Dear Mimmy,
Today was truly, absolutely the worst day ever in Sarajevo. The shooting started around noon. Mommy and I moved into the hall. Daddy was in his office, under our apartment, at the time. We told him on the intercom to run quickly to the downstairs lobby where we'd meet him. We brought Cicko [Zlata's canary] with us. The gunfire was getting worse, and we couldn't get over the wall to the Bobars', so we ran down to our own cellar.

The cellar is ugly, dark, smelly. Mommy, who's terrified of mice, had two fears to cope with. The three of us were in the same corner as the other day. We listened to the pounding shells, the shooting, the thundering noise overhead. We even heard planes. At one moment I realized that this awful cellar was the only place that could save our lives. Suddenly, it started to look almost warm and nice. It was the only way we could defend ourselves against all this terrible shooting. We heard glass shattering in our street. Horrible. I put my fingers in my ears to block out the terrible sounds. I was worried about Cicko. We had left him behind in the lobby. Would he catch cold there? Would something hit him? I was terribly hungry and thirsty. We had left our half-cooked lunch in the kitchen. . . .

This has been the worst, most awful day in my eleven-year-old life. I hope it will be the only one. Mommy and Daddy are very edgy. I have to go to bed.
Ciao!
Zlata

Thursday, May 7, 1992

Dear Mimmy,

I was almost positive the war would stop, but today . . .
Today a shell fell on the park in front of my house, the park
where I used to play and sit with my girlfriends. A lot of
people were hurt. From what I hear, Jaca, Jaca's mother,
Selma, Nina, our neighbor Dado, and who knows how
many other people who happened to be there were
wounded. Dado, Jaca, and her mother have come home
from the hospital; Selma lost a kidney but I don't know
how she is, because she's still in the hospital. **And Nina is
dead.** A piece of shrapnel[7] lodged in her brain and she died.
She was such a sweet, nice little girl. We went to kinder-
garten together, and we used to play together in the park. Is
it possible I'll never see Nina again? Nina, an innocent
eleven-year-old little girl—the victim of a stupid war. I feel
sad. I cry and wonder why? She didn't do anything. A dis-
gusting war has destroyed a young child's life. Nina, I'll
always remember you as a wonderful little girl.
Love, Mimmy,
Zlata

Wednesday, May 13, 1992

Dear Mimmy,

Life goes on. The past is cruel, and that's exactly why we
should forget it.

The present is cruel, too, and I can't forget it. There's
no joking with war. My present reality is the cellar, fear,
shells, fire.

Terrible shooting broke out the night before last. We
were afraid that we might be hit by shrapnel or a bullet, so
we ran over to the Bobars'. We spent all of that night, the
next day, and the next night in the cellar and in Nedo's

---

[7] a piece of bomb, mine, or shell that has exploded

apartment. (Nedo is a refugee from Grbavica. He left his parents and came here to his sister's empty apartment.) We saw terrible scenes on TV. The town in ruins, burning, people and children being killed. It's unbelievable.

The phones aren't working; we haven't been able to find out anything about Grandma and Granddad, Melica, how people in other parts of town are doing. On TV we saw the place where Mommy works, Vodoprivreda, all in flames. It's on the aggressor's[8] side of town (Grbavica). Mommy cried. She's depressed. All her years of work and effort—up in flames. It's really horrible. All around Vodoprivreda there were cars burning, people dying, and nobody could help them. God, why is this happening?

I'm so mad I want to scream and break everything!
Your Zlata

Wednesday, May 27, 1992

Dear Mimmy,
Slaughter! Massacre! Horror! Crime! Blood! Screams! Tears! Despair!
That's what Vaso Miskin Street looks like today. Two shells exploded in the street and one in the market. Mommy was nearby at the time. She ran to Grandma and Granddad's. Daddy and I were beside ourselves because she hadn't come home. I saw some of it on TV but I still can't believe what I actually saw. It's unbelievable. I've got a lump in my throat and a knot in my tummy. **Horrible.** They're taking the wounded to the hospital. It's a madhouse. We kept going to the window hoping to see Mommy, but she wasn't back. They released a list of the dead and wounded. Daddy and I were tearing our hair out. We didn't know what had happened to her. Was she alive? At 4:00, Daddy decided to go and check the hospital. He

---

[8] one who begins an attack or quarrel

got dressed, and I got ready to go to the Bobars', so as not to stay at home alone. I looked out the window one more time and . . . **I saw Mommy running across the bridge.** As she came into the house she started shaking and crying. Through her tears she told us how she had seen dismembered bodies. All the neighbors came because they had been afraid for her. Thank God, Mommy is with us. Thank God.

    A horrible day. Unforgettable.
    Horrible! Horrible!
Your Zlata

Wednesday, June 10, 1992

Dear Mimmy,
At about 11 o'clock last night it started to thunder again. No, not the weather, the shells. We ran over to Nedo's. I fell asleep there, but Mommy and Daddy went back home. There's no electricity. We're cooking on the wood stove in the yard. Everybody is. The whole neighborhood. What luck to have this old stove.

    Daddy and Žika keep fiddling with the radio, listening to the news. They found RFI (Radio France Internationale) in our language. That's at 9 o'clock in the evening and they listen to it regularly. Bojana and I usually play cards, word games or draw something.
Love,
Zlata

Thursday, June 18, 1992

Dear Mimmy,
Today we heard some more sad, sad news. Our country house in Crnotina, a tower that's about 150 years old, has burned down. Like the post office, it disappeared in the flames. I loved it so much. We spent last summer there. I had a wonderful time. I always looked forward to going there. We had redone it so nicely, bought new furniture,

new rugs, put in new windows, given it all our love and warmth, and its beauty was our reward. It lived through so many wars, so many years, and now it's gone. It has burned down to the ground. Our neighbors Žiga, Meho, and Bečir were killed. That's even sadder. Vildana's house also burned down. All the houses burned down. Lots of people were killed. It's terribly sad news.

I keep asking Why? What for? Who's to blame? I ask, but there's no answer. All I know is that we are living in misery. Yes, I know, politics is to blame for it all. I said I wasn't interested in politics, but in order to find out the answer I have to know something about it. They tell me only a few things. I'll probably find out and understand much more one day. Mommy and Daddy don't discuss politics with me. They probably think I'm too young or maybe they themselves don't know anything. They just keep telling me: This will pass—"it has to pass"????????
Your Zlata

Monday, June 22, 1992

Dear Mimmy,
More blood on the streets of Sarajevo. Another massacre. In Tito Street. Three people killed, 35 wounded. Shells fell on Radič, Miss Irbin and Senoa streets. About 15 people were killed in the three streets. I'm worried that something may have happened to Marina's, Marijana's, or Ivana's parents.

These people just go on killing. **Murders!**

I pity them for being so very, very stupid, so servile,[9] for humiliating themselves so much in front of certain people. Terrible!!!!!!
Your Zlata

---

[9] slavelike

Friday, July 3, 1992

Dear Mimmy,

Mommy goes to work at her new office. She goes if there's
no shooting, but we never know when the shelling will
start. It's dangerous to walk around town. It's especially
dangerous to cross our bridge, because snipers shoot at you.
You have to run across. Every time she goes out, Daddy and
I go to the window to watch her run. Mommy says: "I
didn't know the Miljacka (our river) was so wide. You run,
and you run, and you run, and there's no end to the bridge."
That's fear, Mimmy, fear that you'll be hit by something.

Daddy doesn't go to work. The two of us stay at home,
waiting for Mommy. When the sirens go off we worry about
how and when and if she'll get home. Oh, the relief when
she walks in!

Neda came for lunch today. Afterward we played cards.
Neda said something about going to Zagreb. It made
Mommy sad, because they've been friends since childhood.
They grew up together, spent their whole lives together. I
was sad, too, because I love her and I know she loves me.
Zlata

Tuesday, July 7, 1992

Dear Mimmy,

There was no water yesterday, the day before, or the day
before that. It came at around 8:30 this morning and now,
at 10:30, it's slowly disappearing again.

We filled whatever we could find with water and now
have to save on the precious liquid. You have to save on
everything in this war, including water and food. . . .

Thursday, November 19, 1992

Dear Mimmy,

Nothing new on the political front. They are adopting

some resolutions,[10] the "kids" are negotiating, and we are dying, freezing, starving, crying, parting with our friends, leaving our loved ones.

I keep wanting to explain these stupid politics to myself, because it seems to me that politics caused this war, making it our everyday reality. War has crossed out the day and replaced it with horror, and now horrors are unfolding instead of days. It looks to me as though these politics mean Serbs, Croats, and Muslims. But they are all people. They are all the same. They all look like people, there's no difference. They all have arms, legs, and heads; they walk and talk, but now there's "something" that wants to make them different.

Among my girlfriends, among our friends, in our family, there are Serbs and Croats and Muslims. It's a mixed group and I never knew who was a Serb, a Croat, or a Muslim. Now politics has started meddling around. It has put an "S" on Serbs, an "M" on Muslims, and a "C" on Croats; it wants to separate them. And to do so it has chosen the worst, blackest pencil of all—the pencil of war which spells only misery and death.

Why is politics making us unhappy, separating us, when we ourselves know who is good and who isn't? We mix with the good, not with the bad. And among the good there are Serbs and Croats and Muslims, just as there are among the bad. I simply don't understand it. Of course, I'm "young," and politics are conducted by "grown-ups." But I think we "young" would do it better. We certainly wouldn't have chosen war.

The "kids" really are playing, which is why us kids are not playing; we are living in fear, we are suffering, we are not enjoying the sun and flowers, we are not enjoying our childhood. **We are crying.**

---

[10] rules voted on by an official body or assembled group

A bit of philosophizing on my part, but I was alone and felt I could write this to you, Mimmy. You understand me. Fortunately, I've got you to talk to.
And now,
Love,
Zlata

Thursday, December 3, 1992
Dear Mimmy,
Today is my birthday. My first wartime birthday. Twelve years old. Congratulations. Happy birthday to me!

The day started off with kisses and congratulations. First Mommy and Daddy, then everyone else. Mommy and Daddy gave me three Chinese vanity cases—with flowers on them!

As usual there was no electricity. Auntie Melica came with her family (Kenan, Naida, Nihad) and gave me a book. And Braco Lajtner came, of course. The whole neighborhood got together in the evening. I got chocolate, vitamins, a heart-shaped soap (small, orange), a key chain with a picture of Maja and Bojana, a pendant made of a stone from Cyprus, a ring (silver), and earrings (bingo!).

The table was nicely laid, with little rolls, fish-and-rice salad, cream cheese (with Feta),[11] canned corned beef, a pie, and, of course—a birthday cake.

Not how it used to be, but there's a war on. Luckily there was no shooting, so we could celebrate.

It was nice, but something was missing. It's called peace!
Your Zlata

Monday, December 28, 1992
Dear Mimmy,
. . . You know, Mimmy, we've had no water or electricity for ages. When I go out and when there's no shooting it's as if

---

[11] a soft, white goat cheese originally made in Greece

the war were over, but this business with the electricity and water, this darkness, this winter, the shortage of wood and food, brings me back to earth and then I realize that the war is still on. Why? Why on earth don't those "kids" come to some agreement? They really are playing games. And it's us they're playing with.

As I sit writing to you, my dear Mimmy, I look over at Mommy and Daddy. They are reading. They lift their eyes from the page and think about something. What are they thinking about? About the book they are reading, or are they trying to put together the scattered pieces of this war puzzle? I think it must be the latter. Somehow they look even sadder to me in the light of the oil lamp (we have no more wax candles, so we make our own oil lamps). I look at Daddy. He really has lost a lot of weight. The scales say 25 kilos,[12] but looking at him I think it must be more. I think even his glasses are too big for him. Mommy has lost weight too. She's shrunk somehow; the war has given her wrinkles. God, what is this war doing to my parents? They don't look like my old Mommy and Daddy anymore. Will this ever stop? Will our suffering stop so that my parents can be what they used to be—cheerful, smiling, nice-looking?

This stupid war is destroying my childhood; it's destroying my parents' lives. **Why? Stop the war! Peace! I need peace!**

I'm going to play a game of cards with them!
Love from your Zlata

Monday, April 19, 1993

Dear Mimmy,
I've grown, Mimmy. I have nothing to wear. Everything's too small, too tight, too short for me.

I arranged with Braco to see if I could use some of Martina's things; Keka wrote to me and said to take what I need. . . .

---

[12] kilograms; units of weight in the metric system; a kilo is equal to 2.2406 pounds

I remembered what Keka had said in her letter: "Take anything that can brighten up your day, Zlata, and enjoy it if you can, because tomorrow will come. You can be sure of it."

What would brighten up my day is peace; what would brighten up my day is to have them back and to have back everything I've lost.

Ciao!

Zlata

Sunday, April 25, 1993

Dear Mimmy,

I have sad news for you again. Bobo is dead. Auntie Diša's Bobo. He was killed in Melica's garden. It was a sniper. Awful. Everybody was in the garden and the sniper picked him out. What a shame. He was wonderful. He's left behind little Ines, his four-year-old little girl, who is a refugee with her mother.

Auntie Diša is almost out of her mind with grief. She keeps saying: "Maybe he didn't die. It isn't true. My son will come back to me."

Horrible, Mimmy, I can't write to you anymore.

Your Zlata

Friday, September 17, 1993

Dear Mimmy,

The "kids" are negotiating something, signing something. Again giving us hope that this madness will end. There's supposed to be a cease-fire tomorrow; and on September 21 at Sarajevo airport everybody is supposed to sign **for peace.** Will the war stop on the day that marks the change from one season to another???

With all the disappointments I've had with previous truces and signatures, I can't believe it.

I can't believe it because another horrible shell fell today, ending the life of a three-year-old little boy, wounding his sister and mother.

All I know is that the result of their little games is 15,000 dead in Sarajevo, 3,000 of them children, 50,000 permanent invalids, whom I already see in the streets on crutches, in wheelchairs, armless and legless. And I know that there's no room left in the cemeteries and parks to bury the latest victims.

Maybe that's why this madness should stop.
Your Zlata

Sunday, September 19, 1993

Dear Mimmy,
I keep thinking about Sarajevo, and the more I think about it, the more it seems to me that Sarajevo is slowly ceasing to be what it was. So many dead and wounded. Historical monuments destroyed. Treasure troves[13] of books and paintings gone. Century-old trees felled. So many people have left Sarajevo forever. No birds, just the occasional chirping sparrow. A dead city. And the warlords are still negotiating over something, drawing, crossing out, I just don't know for how long. Until September 29? I don't believe it!
Your Zlata

Sunday, October 17, 1993

Dear Mimmy,
Yesterday our friends in the hills reminded us of their presence and that they are now in control and can kill, wound, destroy . . . yesterday was a truly horrible day.

Five hundred and ninety shells. From 4:30 in the morning on, throughout the day. Six dead and fifty-six wounded. That is yesterday's toll. Souk-bunar fared the worst. I don't know how Melica is. They say that half the houses up there are gone.

We went down into the cellar. Into the cold, dark, stupid cellar which I hate. We were there for hours and hours.

---

[13] valuable collections

They kept pounding away. All the neighbors were with us.

Again! Again and again they keep sinking all our boats, taking and burning all our hopes. People said that they wouldn't do it anymore. That there would soon be an end to it, that everything would resolve itself. **That this stupid war will end!**

Oh God, why do they spoil everything? Sometimes I think it would be better if they kept shooting, so that we wouldn't find it so hard when it starts up again. This way, just as you relax, it starts up **again**. I am convinced now that it will never end. Because some people don't want it to, some evil people who hate children and ordinary folk.

I keep thinking that we're alone in this hell, that nobody is thinking of us, nobody is offering us a helping hand. But there are people who are thinking and worrying about us.

Yesterday the Canadian TV crew and Janine came to see how we had survived the mad shelling. That was nice of them. Really kind.

And when we saw that Janine was holding an armful of food, we got so sad we cried. Alexandra came too.

People worry about us, they think about us, but sub-humans want to destroy us. Why? I keep asking myself why?

We haven't done anything. We're innocent. But helpless!
Zlata

REVIEWING AND INTERPRETING

Record your answers to these questions in your personal literature notebook. Follow the directions for each part.

REVIEWING

Try to complete each of these sentences without looking back at the selection.

Recalling Facts

1. Zlata's first hint that something might be wrong was when she
  a. went to school on the first day.
  b. went to M&M's (Martina and Martea's) for Christmas.
  c. got home from school and found her father wearing his uniform.
  d. went apple picking in Crnotina.

Understanding Main Ideas

2. Zlata believed that
  a. Serbs, Croats, and Muslims were really all the same and shouldn't fight.
  b. the war would not affect her or her parents.
  c. the politicians would straighten out the problems in the country.
  d. once peace came, everything would be the same again.

Identifying Sequence

3. Which of the following events took place first?
  a. The country house in Crnotina burned down.
  b. Zlata started fifth grade.
  c. Zlata's friend, Nina, was killed.
  d. The Canadian TV crew and Janine brought Zlata food.

Finding Supporting Details

4. Zlata criticized the politicians for
  a. burning her family's country home.
  b. failing to negotiate a lasting peace.
  c. forcing people to move out of the city.
  d. surrendering to the enemy.

Getting Meaning from Context

5. "They all came to console us and to offer their help." The word *console* means to
a. question.
b. free.
c. warn.
d. comfort.

INTERPRETING

To complete these items, you may look back at the selection if you'd like.

Making Inferences

6. Which is an example of how difficult it was for people to get everyday items?
a. Zlata had to borrow clothing from Martina.
b. Zlata's school closed.
c. Everyone cooked on grills outside.
d. Zlata worried about her family and friends.

Generalizing

7. Zlata can best be described as
a. selfish and angry.
b. bored and unhappy.
c. thoughtful and hopeful.
d. indifferent and depressed.

Recognizing Fact and Opinion

8. Which of the following is a statement of fact?
a. Zlata liked all her classmates at school.
b. Jahorina is the most beautiful mountain in the world.
c. No one in the city understood what the war was about.
d. People standing in line for water risked being shot.

Identifying Cause and Effect

9. Zlata's family and neighbors cooked outside on wood stoves because
a. it was too hot to cook inside.
b. they enjoyed being outside in warm weather.
c. there was no electricity.
d. they had a large supply of wood.

Drawing Conclusions **10.** Before the war in Bosnia, Zlata
a. did not have many friends.
b. was very poor.
c. hated her classes at school.
d. lived a comfortable, normal life.

Now check your answers with your teacher. Study the items you answered incorrectly. What skills are they checking? Talk to your teacher about ways to work on those skills.

Understanding a Diary

You will recall that narrative nonfiction includes autobiographies, biographies, and essays. An *autobiography* is the story of a real person's life written by that person. A *diary* is a type of autobiography. It is a daily record of the events in the writer's life, and it includes the writer's emotions and thoughts. It does not look at the writer's entire life the way some autobiographies do.

Diaries are different from other types of nonfiction in one important way. Autobiographies, biographies, essays, and articles are written for a public audience. That is, the author expects his or her work to be read by others. A diary is written for a private audience—the writer. The author of a diary does not really intend anyone else to read what he or she has written.

If diaries are not meant to be read, why do we read them? Most of us look forward to reading a diary because a diary gives us a peek into a person's thoughts, feelings, and character. In other words, it offers the opportunity to share the writer's innermost thoughts. A diary also gives us a look at a specific time in history through the eyes of the writer and a chance to imagine what it was like to live during that time and in that place.

When we read about other people, we also learn more about ourselves. We can compare our thoughts, feelings, and attitudes with the writer's. From Zlata's diary readers gain an understanding of how war can turn a familiar world upside down.

A diary is told in the first person (*I* or *we*), and the subject of a diary is the writer. In "A Child's Life in Sarajevo," we see Zlata and the events around her as she sees them herself. It is important, however, to examine the different types of information that Zlata reveals. From that information we can decide how much the diary shows about Zlata and the type of person she is.

Many elements combine to make an interesting diary. In the lessons that follow you will learn about three of those elements:

1. **Understanding Setting** Diaries offer an opportunity to experience a different setting—a different time and place.

2. **Understanding Interpretation** The information about events and people are interpreted or understood from the writer's point of view.

3. **Understanding History** Diaries provide a personal sense of history that we don't get from news reports or history books.

LESSON 1 — UNDERSTANDING SETTING

The *setting* is the time and place of the action of a story, play, or poem. Where and when events take place are as important to nonfiction as they are to fiction. To understand setting, readers should be able to form mental images, or pictures, of a certain place. The more successful the writer is in creating these pictures in the mind, the better readers will understand events and people's reactions to them.

As you read Zlata's diary, did you have a clear picture of the place in which she lived? How did the setting affect the events and the way Zlata reacted to them?

Read this passage from Zlata's diary. After you read it, close your eyes and imagine Zlata's country home in Crnotina.

It was wonderful in Crnotina. I like our house (it's really unusual) and the surrounding countryside more and more every time we go. We picked pears, apples, walnuts; we took pictures of a clever little squirrel that stole the walnuts; in the evening we had a barbecue—

my specialty is *ćevapčići* [grilled meat rolls]. Grandma made apple strudel. I collected different leaves for the herbarium and played with Ati.

Autumn has already replaced summer. Slowly but surely it is painting and coloring nature with its brush. The leaves are turning yellow, red, and they are falling. The days are getting shorter and it's colder. Autumn is really nice too! In fact, every season's nice in its own way. Somehow I don't notice and don't feel the beauty of nature when I'm in town the way I do when I'm in Crnotina. In Crnotina it smells good, it caresses me, it calls me into its embrace. I had a really nice rest enjoying and feeling the beauty of nature.

Were you able to visualize, or picture, the setting? Notice how the words that Zlata uses for her descriptions create vivid and exciting images of her surroundings. She uses words that appeal to each of the five senses: sight, hearing, smell, touch, and taste. Were you able to "see" the trees and the colored leaves? Could you "smell" the warm apple strudel as it came out of the oven?

In this passage readers find out what it looks and feels like in the country, but they also gain an understanding of Zlata. It is clear that she loves being in the country. She enjoys picking pears, apples, and walnuts. She delights in watching the seasons change. She loves nature. She says much more than, "Autumn is here, and the trees are beautiful."

EXERCISE 1

Read the following passage from Zlata's diary. Use what you have learned in this lesson to answer the questions that follow it.

Today was truly, absolutely the worst day ever in Sarajevo. The shooting started around noon. Mommy and I moved into the hall. Daddy was in his office, under our apartment, at the time. We told him on the intercom to run quickly to the downstairs lobby where we'd meet him. We brought Cicko [Zlata's canary] with us. The gunfire was getting worse, and we couldn't get over the walls to the Bobars', so we ran down to our own cellar.

The cellar is ugly, dark, smelly. Mommy, who's terrified of mice, had two fears to cope with. The three of us were in the same corner as the other day. We listened to the pounding shells, the shooting, the thundering noise overhead. We even heard planes. At one moment I realized that this awful cellar was the only place that could save our lives. Suddenly, it started to look almost warm and nice. It was the only way we could defend ourselves against all this terrible shooting. We heard glass shattering in our street. Horrible. I put my fingers in my ears to block out the terrible sounds. I was worried about Cicko. We had left him behind in the lobby. Would he catch cold there? Would something hit him? I was terribly hungry and thirsty. We had left our half-cooked lunch in the kitchen. . . .

1. Compare this passage with the earlier passage about the Crnotina countryside. Imagine what it must have been like to huddle in the cellar for hours. To help you compare the two settings, make copies of the cluster maps shown on the next page for Crnotina and for the cellar. Fill in each map with details from the passage that tell what each setting looked, sounded, and felt like.

2. Read the two passages again. What have you learned about Zlata's character from what she has written? What kind of person do you think she is?

Now check your answers with your teacher. Review this lesson if you don't understand why an answer was incorrect.

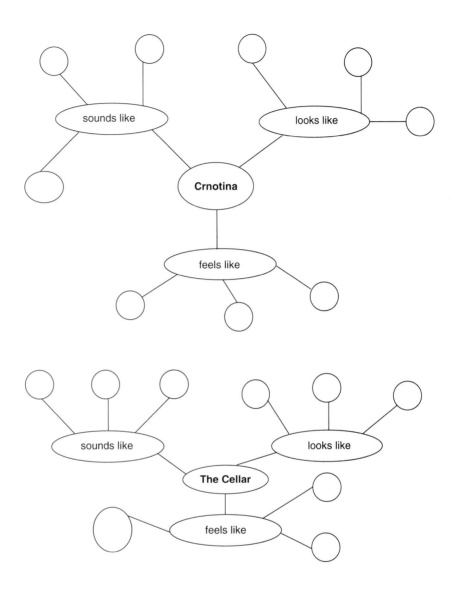

 WRITING ON YOUR OWN 1

In this exercise you will use what you have learned in this lesson to write some notes describing the setting of an event. Follow these steps:

• Copy the graphic organizer below onto a sheet of paper.

EVENT:		
Description of the Setting	**My Interpretation of the Event**	**Description and Interpretation of a Current News Event**
Sight: Hearing: Taste: Touch: Smell:		

• Reread the list you made for Writing: Developing a Diary Entry. Choose one event you listed. In the box at the top of the graphic organizer, write a sentence briefly describing the event.
• In the column below the heading "Description of the Setting" write some brief notes describing the setting in which the event took place. Where were you when the event occurred? Were you at home, in school, inside, or outside? Was anyone else with you? What sounds did you hear? What did you smell? Was it cloudy, raining, or sunny? Use descriptive words in your notes. Try to use words that appeal to most or all of the five senses: sight, hearing, smell, taste, and touch.
• When you have finished writing your descriptive notes, reread them. Would more details create a more vivid image of the setting?
• Save your graphic organizer. You will add to it in the next lesson.

LESSON 2 | UNDERSTANDING INTERPRETATION

You have most likely been in a situation in which a person has said something to you that you understood as something else. Maybe you thought someone was upset with you when he or she was really just tired or busy. How you view a particular situation is your interpretation of that situation. An *interpretation* is one person's view of the meaning of certain words, events, or actions.

Imagine how a person who tries out for and gets a part in the school play interprets the event. How do you think that person feels? Now, imagine how the person who tries out and doesn't get the part interprets the same event. How do you think he or she describes the event? If they both record the event in their diaries, the descriptions of the tryout will be quite different. Each person will interpret the event differently on the basis of differing experiences.

In a diary, the writer interprets events according to his or her point of view. Readers see other people and events through the writer's eyes. In her diary entries, Zlata provides insight into her feelings and her own interpretation of how the war affected people in Croatia.

In this passage from her diary Zlata wonders about politics and how much her parents know about the war.

Today we heard some more sad, sad news. Our country house in Crnotina . . . has burned down. . . . It has burned down to the ground. Our neighbors Žiga, Meho, and Bečir were killed. That's even sadder. Vildana's house also burned down. All the houses burned down. Lots of people were killed. It's terribly sad news.

I keep asking Why? What for? Who's to blame? I ask, but there's no answer. All I know is that we are living in misery. Yes, I know, politics is to blame for it all. I said I wasn't interested in politics, but in order to find out the answer I have to know something about it. They tell me only a few things. I'll probably find out and understand much more one day. Mommy and Daddy don't discuss politics with me. They probably think I'm too young or maybe they themselves don't know anything. They just keep telling me: This will pass— "it has to pass"????????

Zlata does not understand why people are killing each other. She thinks that either her parents don't tell her all they know or they don't know the facts themselves. Zlata's interpretation becomes the lens through which readers see the people and events. What do you think Zlata's parents know about the war? Would their interpretation be different from Zlata's? Why might Zlata's parents want to keep certain details of the war from her?

EXERCISE 2

Read this passage from the diary. Then use what you have learned in this lesson to answers the questions that follow.

I'm not going to school. All the schools in Sarajevo are closed. There's danger hiding in these hills above Sarajevo. But I think things are slowly calming down. The heavy shelling and explosions have stopped. There's occasional gunfire, but it quickly falls silent. Mommy and Daddy aren't going to work. They're buying food in huge quantities. Just in case, I guess. God forbid!

Still, it's very tense. Mommy is beside herself, Daddy tries to calm her down. Mommy has long conversations on the phone. She calls, other people call, the phone is in constant use.

1. Zlata seems to think that things in Sarajevo are calming down. What do you think her parents' views are? What details in the passage support your answer?

2. How do you interpret the fact that Zlata's mother spends so much time on the phone?

Now check your answers with your teacher. Review this lesson if you don't understand why an answer was incorrect.

 WRITING ON YOUR OWN 2

In this lesson you learned about understanding interpretation. Now write some notes that give your interpretation, or view, of your chosen event. Follow these steps.

- Look at the graphic organizer you started in Writing on Your Own 1. Reread the notes you wrote describing the setting.
- In the column below the heading "My Interpretation of the Event," write some brief notes describing the event from your point of view. Perhaps you wrote about something that happened in class, at lunch, at gym, at home, or at a friend's house. Think about what happened and how you interpreted the event. For example, imagine that in the lunchroom one day a bully took someone's dessert and ate it. Others laughed, but you felt sorry for the person whose dessert had been taken. In your notes express *your* thoughts and feelings.
- Save your graphic organizer. You will add to it in the next lesson.

LESSON 3 — UNDERSTANDING HISTORY

People often think of history as a list of facts and dates to remember. For example, if you were watching the evening news and heard a report about the war in Croatia, it probably would have little meaning for you. When an event in history is presented in a diary through the eyes of someone who lived through it, however, it comes alive. You begin to understand the impact of the event on people's lives. In other words, you identify with what the person is thinking and feeling.

In this passage from her diary, Zlata makes a war in a far-off place seem very real. Readers get a sense of what the war is really doing to people.

> I was almost positive the war would stop, but today . . . Today a shell fell on the park in front of my house, the park where I used to play and sit with my girlfriends. A lot of people were hurt. From what I hear, Jaca, Jaca's mother, Selma, Nina, our neighbor Dado, and who knows how many other people who happened to be there were wounded. Dado, Jaca, and her mother have come home from the hospital; Selma lost a kidney but I don't know how she is, because she's still in the hospital. **And Nina is dead.** A piece of shrapnel lodged in her brain and she died. She was such a sweet, nice little girl. We went to kindergarten together, and we used to play together in the park. Is it possible I'll never see Nina again? Nina, an innocent eleven-year-old little girl—the victim of a stupid war. I feel sad. I cry and wonder why? She didn't do anything. A disgusting war has destroyed a young child's life. Nina, I'll always remember you as a wonderful little girl.
> Love, Mimmy,
> Zlata

Now imagine what a TV news report would sound like: "There was fighting again in Sarajevo. An artillery shell hit a park. Several people were killed and wounded." This typical news report is impersonal, presenting just the essential facts. After reading Zlata's account of the shelling, however, readers are able to put themselves in Zlata's place. They begin to get a very real sense of how the event affects the lives of those who live in Sarajevo.

EXERCISE 3

Read this passage from the diary. Use what you have learned in this lesson to answer the questions that follow it.

Life goes on. The past is cruel, and that's exactly why we should forget it.

The present is cruel, too, and I can't forget it. There's no joking with war. My present reality is the cellar, fear, shells, fire.

Terrible shooting broke out the night before last. We were afraid that we might be hit by shrapnel or a bullet, so we ran over to the Bobars'. We spent all of that night, the next day, and the next night in the cellar and in Nedo's apartment. . . . We saw terrible scenes on TV. The town in ruins, burning, people and children being killed. It's unbelievable.

The phones aren't working, and we haven't been able to find out anything about Grandma and Granddad, Melica, how people in other parts of town are doing. On TV we saw the place where Mommy works, Vodoprivreda, all in flames. It's on the aggressor's side of town. . . . Mommy cried. She's depressed. All her years of work and effort—up in flames. It's really horrible. All around Vodoprivreda there are cars burning, people dying, and nobody could help them. God, why is this happening?

I'm so mad I want to scream and break everything!

1. What emotions is Zlata experiencing? Why does she want to scream and break everything?

2. Imagine that you are a news reporter. How will you report the events that Zlata is describing?

Now check your answers with your teacher. Review this lesson if you don't understand why an answer was incorrect.

 WRITING ON YOUR OWN 3

In this exercise you will use what you have learned about understanding historical events to add something to your diary—a current news event. Follow these steps:

- Review the graphic organizer you used in Writing on Your Own 1 and 2. In the organizer you wrote notes describing the setting of an event and how you interpreted that event.
- Now you are going to think of a current news event that you will mention briefly in the diary entry you are preparing to write. Choose a news event of the past day or two that caught your interest, one that you gave some thought. Perhaps it was news about a local happening—a new shopping-mall opening or a great win for a local sports team. Or perhaps it was a major national news event. If you can't think of such an event, look through the newspaper for some ideas.

- In the column below the heading "Description and Interpretation of a News Event," write a few notes briefly describing the event and expressing some of your thoughts and feelings about it.
- Be sure to save your graphic organizer. You will use it for your final writing activity in this unit.

DISCUSSION GUIDES

1. In a diary you learn about the writer's personal thoughts and feelings. The way that person talks about events or people tells about his or her character. In a small group discuss what conclusions you can draw about Zlata's character from what she says in her diary. Share your conclusions with the other groups. Are their conclusions different from yours? If so, why?

2. When we read a diary, we see all the events and people as they are viewed by the writer. Zlata thinks about the war, her friends, and school. Imagine that you are one of Zlata's parents. As a class discuss what you think they are worried about? Do you think Zlata's parents are telling her all they know about the war? Why or why not?

3. In her diary entry for March 5, 1992, Zlata refers to the politicians as "kids." In a small group discuss what Zlata and others might mean when they refer to the politicians as "kids." Share your observations with the rest of the class.

WRITE A DIARY ENTRY

In this unit you have learned that there are many elements that combine to make an interesting diary. Now you will use what you have learned to write your own diary entry.

Follow these steps to complete your diary entry. If you have questions about the writing process, refer to Using the Writing Process (page 217).

- Gather and review the following pieces of writing you did for this unit: 1) A list of events and sentences describing them, 2) the graphic organizer you filled in with notes describing the setting of the event you chose, your interpretation of that event, and a brief description and interpretation of a current news event.
- As you write your diary entry remember to use the first person (*I, me, we,* and *us*). Your diary tells about *your* interpretations, or views, of people and events—your thoughts and your feelings.
- Begin by writing the day and date of your entry. Then write a paragraph describing the setting. Be sure that your description creates a vivid image of the setting by using descriptive words that appeal to most or all of the five senses.
- Next, write a paragraph in which you give your interpretation of the event—expressing your thoughts and feelings about it. Through your thoughts and feelings, you reveal your character—the kind of person you are.
- Finally, close your diary entry by writing a paragraph briefly describing a current news event and your thoughts and feelings about it.
- When you have completed a draft of your diary, read it to classmates in a small group. Ask for their comments and any suggestions they might have for improving it. If you agree with any suggested changes, revise your diary entry accordingly.
- Proofread your final draft for errors in spelling, grammar, punctuation, and capitalization. Make a final copy and save it in your writing portfolio.

Analyzing Nonfiction

River Creatures

An excerpt from *The Land I Lost* by Huynh Quang Nhuong

INTRODUCTION

BUILDING
BACKGROUND

The United States fought a bloody and difficult war in Vietnam from 1965 until 1973. Before the war Americans knew very little of Vietnam or its people. When the war ended, most people in the United States soon stopped thinking about that small Southeast Asian nation half way around the world.

Vietnam is a beautiful country with a long and rich history. For many years, however, the entire country was a war zone where various military and political groups fought for control of the government. The selection you are about to read is taken from a book written by a Vietnamese man who left his native land at the end of the terrible war there. "River Creatures" comes from the book *The Land I Lost*. In his book Huynh Quang Nhuong wrote about his happy boyhood in a small rural village in the days before the war came. The author chose the title for his book to show that he cannot return to his native land because he is an enemy of the present government. The title also says that he knows that the rural country life he remembers from his boyhood has been destroyed forever. Even if he could return to Vietnam, he could never have that simple, happy

These Vietnamese children are riding water buffaloes. The buffaloes work hard in rice fields like those pictured here, but they don't mind giving rides.

life again. He writes, "The land I love was lost to me forever. These stories are my memories."

Huynh Quang Nhuong lived in a very small village near the
Vietnam-Laos border. His village was located on the bank of
a large river, with deep jungle on one side and a chain of
high mountains on the other. Around the village, fields of
rice, sweet potatoes, mustard, eggplant, tomatoes, hot pep-
pers, and corn stretched into the distance in all directions.
Nhuong's early life was spent working with his family in the
fields, tending the village's herd of water buffalo, and in the
activities of small boys everywhere—fishing, playing games,
roaming around, and getting into mischief.

The Land I Lost is a very popular book. It has won several awards for juvenile nonfiction. (Juvenile nonfiction is
written especially for readers about your own age.) Readers
have especially enjoyed the author's exciting and amusing
stories about the feats of Tank, his family's brave and intelligent water buffalo. A water buffalo is a huge, powerful
animal with long, thick, pointed horns. In Vietnam, water
buffalo are used as work animals.

The author was a young man when the United States
became involved in the civil war between North and South
Vietnam. He was drafted into the South Vietnamese Army,
wounded in battle, and permanently paralyzed. When South
Vietnam was defeated, he came to the United States for further medical treatment. He has remained here ever since.

The lessons that follow "River Creatures" focus on analyzing several important elements of nonfiction.

We will examine the characteristics of the different
types of nonfiction, the different purposes writers have for

writing nonfiction, and how information and ideas in non-fiction are organized into main ideas and supporting details.

WRITING: DEVELOPING AN ANALYSIS

At the end of this unit, you will write an analysis of a selection from one of the first six units in this book. An *analysis* is a careful examination of something in order to bring out its essential elements. The following suggestions will help you get started:

- Open to the table of contents at the front of your book. On a sheet of paper list the titles of the reading selections in Units 1 to 6.
- Decide what *type* of nonfiction you think each selection is: expository nonfiction (gives factual information) or narrative nonfiction (reads like fiction but tells about real people, places, and events). Write your choice beside each title. You may look at the selection to help you decide.
- Decide what *form* of nonfiction each selection is: autobiography, biography, narrative essay, or article. Write your choice beside its title. You may look back at the selection.

AS YOU READ

Think about these questions as you read "River Creatures." They will help you analyze the selection.

- What kind of nonfiction is "River Creatures"?
- What is the author's purpose for writing the selection?
- What is the central idea of the selection?
- What details in the selection support the central idea?

River Creatures

An excerpt from *The Land I Lost* by Huynh Quang Nhuong

When my father did not need Tank to till[1] the rice fields during the rainy season, I liked to ride on his back and look for an otters' party. There were many otters living on the riverbanks in front of our hamlet[2] because fish were plentiful in the deep river. Normally the otters lived in twos. But once in a while they all gathered together, caught a great number of fish, and threw them up on the riverbank. Then they all sat down around the fish and ate them. We called this unusual gathering an otters' party.

One day my cousin and I thought up a plan to capture the otters' fish. It would be hard to do because if the otters saw people approaching to try and take their fish, they jumped back into the river and took all the fish with them. But otters did not worry about other animals, so I decided that because Tank's back was wide and high above the ground I could lie flat on his back and approach an otters' party without attracting their attention. To make detection[3] of me even more difficult, I would wear clothes

---

[1] to prepare the soil for planting

[2] a small village

[3] a finding out; discovery

that blended in as much as possible with the color of Tank's back. I would also carry a sturdy stick to scare the otters away in case they turned on me. I had to take this last pre-caution because I knew that otters, when gathered in a large group, had attacked people who passed by them in small boats.

A few days later I spotted an otters' party on the river-bank. I found a good stick and climbed onto Tank's back. After I showed Tank the direction I wanted him to go, I lay face down and let him carry me to the party. When Tank was about three meters[4] from the group, I slid down to the ground and chased all the otters into the river. That day I caught them thoroughly by surprise, and I got twenty-four fish, all different kinds, and most of them still intact[5] and fresh.

After that I repeated my raids as often as I could and usually with great success. But one day, after I had surprised the otters and put all the fish on Tank's back, I noticed that one female did not leave. She just swam up and down the river and seemed very anxious to return to where I was. Sensing something unusual, I carefully looked around and discovered three otter cubs in a very deep, narrow hole under a thick thistle bush. I was very excited. Otter cubs were priceless, for one could train an otter cub to catch as many fish as one wanted.

When I had squeezed myself into the hole and had almost reached the cubs, the mother otter came up behind me and bit my toes, very hard! It was so painful that I had to crawl out of the hole as quickly as possible and shake her off. The mother otter jumped back into the river, but when I crawled into the hole again, I received the same painful bite on my toes. Suddenly, I came up with an idea. I took some mud from the riverbank and wrote on Tank's back,

---

[4] about 3.28 yards

[5] undamaged; whole

Otter cubs—come quickly. Then I gave Tank a little tap on the back and said, "Go." Tank trotted straight home.

When Tank arrived home my parents saw the fish he carried, but no me. They panicked. Then they discovered the message on Tank's back, and they were very happy. My cousin and Tank soon returned to where I was. My cousin prevented the mother otter from biting me while I took the three cubs out of the hole, one by one.

We sold two of the cubs at the marketplace to two rich merchants, and kept the third one to train to catch fish for us.

The cub we kept quickly learned its job, but we always kept it in an iron cage for fear that it would run away from us. Unfortunately, when I caught the cub its eyes had already opened. If it had just been born and its eyes had not yet opened, we would have been the first beings it saw, and it would have considered us as its parents and remained with us for the rest of its life.

Afterward whenever we wanted fish we just brought our otter to the riverbank, tied it to a long rope to prevent it from escaping, and let it dive into the river. When it caught a fish it surfaced and gave the fish to us.

Since it was always easy for us to get fish, we gave them to friends whenever they wanted any. Sometimes, when we had free days, we let our otter fish all day long. It caught a great number of fish, which we then dried and sent to our relatives who weren't as lucky as we to have a trained otter for a fisherman.

In the river in front of our hamlet there lived a type of catfish that weighed more than one hundred kilos[6] when fully grown. Gourmets[7] sought them, but they were difficult to catch because they often broke the fishline or tore up

---

[6] about 220 pounds

[7] people who are expert in judging and choosing fine foods

the fishnet. We called them white catfish in order to distinguish them from black catfish which were darker and smaller.

To catch white catfish we used a squirrel or a big frog as bait. We couldn't use fishing poles made of light bamboo trees because they would break. And big, heavy poles were too tiring to hold. Thus a fisherman who wanted to catch a white catfish just held the fishline firmly in his hands. When the catfish bit, the fisherman held the line for a while. If the line did not break and the catfish tired, he slowly pulled it to the riverbank and used a big net to pull it onto dry ground.

One day I left Tank and the other buffaloes grazing near the river while I talked with a friend of my family's. He was old and could not do hard work in the field, so he fished for white catfish to help out his family. I had just finished saying that if a fish took the bait, I would help him, when I saw his face turn pink and his hands shake very hard. Immediately I jumped next to him, grabbed the line, and started pulling.

The fish fought back like a devil, and one of its powerful jerks almost dragged both of us into the river. I yelled to Tank to come and help us.

Tank came quickly. We tied the fishline to his horns and signaled him to walk backward. Tank lowered his head and pulled with all his strength. Luckily, the line held, and Tank dragged the fish closer and closer to shore. Suddenly we saw a huge white catfish jump into the air and then fall back into the water with a tremendous splash. Tank kept pulling and the old man kept yelling, "That's right, son. That's right, son." Moments later we saw the head of the fish come out of the water, then the body, and finally the tail.

When the entire fish was on the riverbank, we stopped Tank and untied the line from his horns. Our old friend was so happy that he jumped up and down like a child. He said that without me and Tank, he knew that the catfish would have gotten away from him. Then we brought Tank closer to the fish so that he could see it clearly. Tank looked at the fish and pricked up his ears in a funny way.

My old friend called it a day, because he had made a big catch and he wanted to go home immediately to show his family. But the fish was too heavy for him to carry. Although it was still early, I decided to bring the herd home so that Tank could help our friend carry the fish.

I told our friend that we should load the fish on Tank's back. He was very happy with the idea, but said that first he had to cut off the fish's pectoral fins.[8] He explained to me that each pectoral fin has a spine[9] with venom[10] in it that made a cut from the fin very painful. He took a knife out of his pocket, cut off the two pectoral fins, and thereby prevented Tank from being hurt.

When we arrived at my house, where I left the herd, the old friend wanted to give my parents part of the fish. But my parents refused his offer, telling him that our otter caught all the fish we needed. They said he should keep the whole fish and sell it at the marketplace, where he would get a good price for such a delicacy.[11]

Tank and I accompanied our friend to his house. When we arrived, his family was very happy to see the big fish. The old man kept repeating how wildly the fish had fought and how helpful Tank and I had been.

Soon all his children got busy. Several carried the fish inside, one prepared tea for him, and another hung his fishing line on the wall. When the boys and girls were tired of looking at the fish, they surrounded Tank and asked me endless questions about him: Why was Tank's stomach so big? Was he pregnant? Why were the hairs at the end of his tail longer than those on his head? And so on.

---

[8] either of a pair of fish fins, usually just behind the gills

[9] a sharp, bony part of the fin

[10] poison

[11] something that is pleasing to eat and is considered rare

My friend's wife wanted me to stay for dinner, but I refused because my parents had told me to be back as soon as possible. My mother wanted to use Tank to draw some water from the well. But as I said good-bye, my friend's wife made sure I didn't refuse a piece of cake to eat on the way home, and a lump of brown sugar for Tank. Tank was very fond of brown sugar—more than he was of fishing, I think!

From the time Tank helped our old friend to get the white catfish, I had considered the idea of catching golden eels with Tank's help. There were two kinds of golden eels living in our area—one kind had bulging eyes, the other had beady eyes. Both were very much sought after because their meat was excellent. These eels, when matured, reached two meters[12] in length and weighed about five kilos.[13]

The eels lived in muddy ditches that brought water to the fruit gardens, the banana groves, and the coconut groves when the level of the water in the river in front of our hamlet was high. They hid in deep holes that they dug in the hard clay soil beneath the mud of the ditch, usually near a tree planted on the border of the ditch. The roots of the tree were a natural barrier against intruders, and when an eel coiled its body around the root of a tree, it was almost impossible to pull it out. Each eel's nest had several openings to allow it to escape in case of danger, and inside a nest there were many zigzag corners, which allowed an eel to hook its body around a corner and resist someone's trying to pull it out by its head or tail.

Eels lay constantly in ambush near the main entrance of their nest, waiting for prey to pass by—fish, shrimp, crabs, even baby ducks if a mother duck was foolish enough to lead her young brood over an eel's nest. Then the eel would shoot out of its nest like an arrow, snap up a baby duck, pull it down into its nest, and swallow it moments later.

[12] about 2.28 yards

[13] about 11 pounds

Sometimes an eel even tried to attack an adult duck if food was scarce. It would bite the duck's foot and try to pull the frightened fowl down into the nest where it would drown. The duck might survive if someone heard it quack and rushed to rescue it, but it would often lose one foot because the teeth of a golden eel are very sharp.

One could lure[14] an eel with almost any kind of bait, but we used earthworms because they were easy to find. We would dangle the worm at the nest's entrance, and sooner or later the eel would come out and bite the bait. We allowed the eel to swallow the bait far down into its stomach, instead of pulling the line right away, for if we pulled the line too soon we would only succeed in tearing off the eel's jaw during the struggle to pull it out of its nest. But with a hook in its stomach, it could not get away—no matter how hard it tried. Sooner or later, unless the fishing line broke, we would drag the eel out of its nest, dead or alive.

In our hamlet, whenever an eel was hooked, the children of the neighborhood had a good time. They ran out of their houses when they heard the yell for help. Two or three boys would help pull out the eel, and everyone else yelled or laughed. Sometimes adults came to help too, if they were not busy. It took at least one hour to pull the eel out of its nest, and by this time, it was usually dead.

But a live eel got a better price than a dead one in the market, and since Tank had easily succeeded in pulling the white catfish out of the river for our old friend, I came up with the idea of letting him drag eels out of their nests for me. If he could pull an eel out quickly, I had a better chance to get the eel alive instead of dead.

First I had to find an eel's nest, but this was not difficult. One can know roughly the location of a nest by listening carefully to the sound an eel makes when it snaps at a victim. The sound made by its closing jaws is similar to that of

---

[14] to attract

a loud click and can be heard clearly from thirty or forty meters[15] away, especially at night.

After finding the general area of a nest, I pinpointed the exact location by examining the mud. The mud around the main entrance of the nest is always more disturbed than the rest. Then I tied the end of a fishing line to Tank's horns and made the bait jump up and down on the mud covering the hole. The eel stuck its head out of the mud first, saw the bait clearly, snapped it up, and returned to its nest below. I loosened the line to let the eel swallow the bait into its stomach, then I signaled Tank to pull. Despite his tremendous strength, Tank needed quite a bit of effort to pull the eel out of its nest. But it was the most exciting sight to see the wagging head of the eel stick out of the mud first, and then its big, trembling golden body come slowly out of the hole. When the eel was on dry ground, it yanked, turned, and squirmed like an earthworm attacked by a swarm of fire ants.

Using this method, I caught several big eels; none of them could resist Tank more than fifty counts. When Tank started pulling, I counted, One, two, three . . . Some strong eels reached forty-five, but the weaker ones were already on dry ground, wriggling, when I had not yet reached twenty. Often, when an eel had taken the bait, I yelled to my friends to come to see Tank's work. When everybody arrived, I signaled Tank to pull. Some of my friends counted with me while the others yelled, clapped their hands, or cheered loudly for Tank.

It was difficult to tell whether Tank enjoyed fishing for eels as much as we did, but he always accomplished his task extremely well.

---

[15] about 33 to 44 yards

REVIEWING AND INTERPRETING

Record your answers to these questions in your personal literature notebook. Follow the directions for each part.

REVIEWING Try to complete each of these sentences without looking back at the selection.

Recalling Facts
1. Tank was mainly used to
a. catch otters.
b. pull eels from their nests.
c. till the rice fields.
d. help the fishermen.

Understanding Main Ideas
2. Another title for this selection might be
a. The Otter Hunt.
b. Tank Helps with the Fishing.
c. How to Catch a White Catfish.
d. A Trip to the Marketplace.

Identifying Sequence
3. The first step in catching a golden eel was to
a. tie the end of a fishing line to Tank's horns.
b. find the eel's nest.
c. dangle bait in front of the eel's nest.
d. yank the eel out of its nest.

Getting Meaning from Context
4. Otter cubs were priceless, for one could train an otter cub to catch as many fish as one wanted." The word *priceless* means
a. very strong.
b. very shy.
c. very valuable.
d. very playful.

Finding Supporting Details

5. An example of why eels are so difficult to pull from their nests is that
   a. they wrap themselves around a tree root.
   b. it is impossible to find their nests.
   c. they move very quickly.
   d. they have very sharp teeth.

INTERPRETING

To complete these items, you may look back at the selection if you'd like.

Making Inferences

6. The people in Nhuong's village survived mostly by
   a. raising otter cubs.
   b. eating eels.
   c. shopping at the marketplace.
   d. fishing and farming.

Generalizing

7. Which statement best describes how the author felt about the hamlet where he grew up?
   a. He enjoyed his life in the hamlet.
   b. He could not wait to move to a big city.
   c. He was very unhappy there.
   d. He was bored by a life of farming and fishing.

Recognizing Fact and Opinion

8. Which of the following is a statement of opinion?
   a. White catfish can weigh more than 200 pounds when fully grown.
   b. Tank liked brown sugar more than he liked fishing.
   c. Many otters lived near the author's hamlet.
   d. The author's otter caught many fish.

Identifying Cause and Effect

9. It is better to catch an otter cub before its eyes open because then
   a. it cannot find its mother.
   b. it can catch more fish.
   c. it will not remember where its home is.
   d. it thinks the first beings it sees are its parents.

Drawing Conclusions

10. Drawing on the events in this essay, you can conclude that
   a. Tank is a dangerous animal.
   b. the author believed in teamwork and helping others.
   c. the author was afraid of eels.
   d. the author only wanted to fish.

Now check your answers with your teacher. Study the items you answered incorrectly. What skills are they checking? Talk with your teacher about ways to work on those skills.

Analyzing Nonfiction

In Unit 4 you read the article "Houston, We've Had a Problem." You will recall that it tells the story of *Apollo 13*'s unsuccessful and nearly fatal attempt to reach the moon. Nearly nine months earlier, *Apollo 11* had been successful and made the first manned lunar, or moon, landing on July 20, 1969. Part of the mission of *Apollo 11*'s crew was to bring back rock and dirt samples so that scientists on earth could analyze them. To *analyze* something is to examine it carefully in order to reveal its essential elements. By analyzing parts of the moon, scientists sought to learn more about the moon itself. Have you ever taken something apart to see how it works—perhaps a clock, a watch, or a toy? By studying the parts that make up something, we can gain a greater understanding of the object itself.

In a way, you are like those scientists. But instead of examining moon rocks to gain a better understanding of the moon, you have been examining some elements, or parts, of nonfiction in order to understand it better. In earlier units in this book, you studied many different kinds of nonfiction, the purposes authors have for writing nonfiction, and the writing techniques they use to accomplish those purposes. You also studied ways that authors of nonfiction organize their thoughts and ideas.

In the following lessons, we will reexamine some of these essential elements and characteristics. We will focus on these:

1. **Analyzing Types of Nonfiction** Nonfiction tells about real people, places, and events but in a variety of different ways. Authors tell their stories or present their information, ideas, and opinions through different forms of nonfiction, and through different styles of writing.

2. **Analyzing Author's Purpose** Nonfiction authors write for one of several purposes. Identifying the author's

purpose—*why* he or she wrote—and determining whether the author achieved that purpose is particularly important when reading nonfiction.

3. **Analyzing Main Ideas and Details** Authors of nonfiction organize their information and ideas by establishing one or more main ideas and supporting them with details. When reading nonfiction, it's important to identify the author's main ideas and to be able to determine whether those ideas have been supported by details.

LESSON 1 ANALYZING THE FORMS OF NONFICTION

In the first unit in this book, you learned that nonfiction is writing that tells about real people, places, and events. This is a simple definition and one that is easy to remember, but as you've discovered, the study of nonfiction is more complex than its definition suggests.

Nonfictional writing comes in many different forms. Nonfiction can appear as a serious article about tornadoes, a narrative essay about life on a farm, an instructive article on how to build a birdhouse, a biography of Thomas Edison, your science textbook, or even someone's diary. Articles, essays, biographies, diaries—how can you distinguish one from the other? Fortunately, each form of nonfiction has its own characteristics.

In Unit 2 you learned that there are two main types of nonfiction: expository nonfiction and narrative nonfiction. *Expository nonfiction* gives factual information. Examples of expository nonfiction are history and science textbooks, and magazine and newspaper articles. An example of expository nonfiction that you read in this book is "Where Is Cyberspace?" Can you think of another example in this book?

Narrative nonfiction reads like fiction except that it tells about real people, places, and events. Some examples of narrative nonfiction are autobiographies, biographies, and essays. "Another April," a selection you read in this book, is narrative nonfiction. Can you think of another example?

Each of the different forms of expository and narrative nonfiction have unique characteristics that help to identify them—for example, an *article* is a nonfiction work that informs or explains a subject to the reader. "Where Is Cyberspace?" is an article. An *autobiography* is a story of a real person's life written by that person; a *biography* is a story about a real person's life written by someone else. You have read a selection in this book taken from a biography and another selection that is not a complete autobiography but has most of the characteristics of one. Can you name those two selections?

Two other kinds of narrative nonfiction that you read and studied in this book are the essay and the diary. An *essay* is a brief piece of nonfiction that expresses a person's opinion or view about a particular subject. In this book your study focused on the *narrative essay*—an essay that tells about a real-life experience in the form of a story. Which selections in this book were narrative essays? You have also learned about the diary. A *diary* is a daily record of the events in the writer's life and includes the writer's emotions and thoughts. Which selection in this book is a diary?

When you analyze a piece of nonfiction to determine its form, examine its characteristics. They will help you identify it. Read the following passage from one of the selections in this book. As you read, look for clues that will help you identify which form of nonfiction it is.

Computers can be plugged into each other (this is called a *network*), so you can log into computer 1, but play games stored on computer number 5 and computer number 30! The red door might lead to a second room, my friend's room. Her computer doesn't need to be in the same real-life room, either. Computers can be linked with different kinds of wiring, like fiber optic cable and telephone wire.

Did you recognize that this passage is expository nonfiction and that it is from an article. An analysis of its characteristics tells you that. The passage gives factual information and explains a subject to the reader.

The next passage is a different form of nonfictional writing. Read through the excerpt and try to determine its form. Consider any characteristics in the writing that might help you do this.

When the little girl disappeared from view, McWilliams walked through her St. Louis rooming-house hallway to the backyard. There clustered around the rickety porch, stood her wooden washtubs. Years later she remembered the moment: "As I bent over the washboard and looked at my arms buried in the soap-suds, I said to myself, 'What are you going to do when you grow old and your back gets stiff?' This set me to thinking, but with all my thinking, I couldn't see how I, a poor washerwoman, was going to better my condition."

Did you recognize the excerpt as a passage from the biography of Madam C. J. Walker? Writers of biography want to accomplish two things in their work: they want to provide the facts of a subject's life, and they want to make the subject come to life for the reader. Since facts don't always bring a subject to life, a biographer will narrate events from the subject's life to give the reader a sense of the individual's character. What does this incident about Madam C. J. Walker tell you about her character?

EXERCISE 1

Read the following passage from a selection in this book. Use what you have learned in this lesson to answer the questions that follow it.

Monday, September 2, 1991
Behind me—a long, hot summer and the happy days of summer holidays; ahead of me—a new school year. I'm starting fifth grade. I'm looking forward to seeing my friends at school, to being together again. Some of them I haven't seen since the day the school bell rang, marking the end of term. I'm glad we'll be together again, and share all the worries and joys of going to school.

1. What form of narrative nonfiction is this passage? Give reasons for your answer.

2. What writing style does the author use in this passage?

Now check your answers with your teacher. Review this lesson if you don't understand why an answer was incorrect.

 WRITING ON YOUR OWN 1

In this exercise you will use what you have learned in this lesson to analyze a selection to determine what form of nonfiction it is. Follow these steps:

• Look at the list of titles you wrote for Writing: Developing an Analysis. Recalling what you have studied in Lesson 1 in this unit, check your list to see whether you have accurately identified the form of nonfiction each selection is.
• Choose one of the six selections on your list to be the subject of your analysis. Analyze the selection carefully this

time to be certain of its form. Reread the selection if necessary.

- Write a paragraph telling what form of nonfiction the selection is. Give reasons or cite examples to support your conclusions.

LESSON 2 | ANALYZING AUTHOR'S PURPOSE

In Unit 3 you learned about the five general purposes authors have for writing: to inform, to instruct, to entertain, to express an opinion, or to persuade readers to do or believe something. You also learned that authors sometimes have more than one purpose in mind when they write, but usually one purpose is the most important. What do you think is Nhuong's purpose for writing?

The events in "River Creatures" are the author's memories of his boyhood. He is writing to make a record of those memories for others to read, so one of his purposes is to inform—to give readers information about himself, his hamlet, the people who live there and their way of life.

Read this passage from the essay. As you read, decide what Nhuong's purpose is in writing it.

In the river in front of our hamlet there lived a type of catfish that weighed more than one hundred kilos when fully grown. Gourmets sought them, but they were difficult to catch because they often broke the fishline or tore up the fishnet. We called them white catfish in order to distinguish them from black catfish which were darker and smaller.

To catch white catfish we used a squirrel or a big frog as bait. We couldn't use fishing poles made of light bamboo trees because they would break. And big, heavy poles were too tiring to hold. Thus a fisherman who wanted to catch a white catfish just held the fishline firmly in his hands. When the catfish bit, the fisherman held the line for a while. If the line did not break and the catfish tired, he slowly pulled it to the riverbank and used a big net to pull it onto dry ground.

If you decided the author's purpose is to inform, you are right. In this excerpt, Nhuong wants to inform his audience how very difficult it is to catch a white catfish so that later in the story readers will appreciate what a great feat it is for Tank to land the fish. Besides their general purposes for writing—to inform, instruct, entertain, express an opinion, or persuade—authors often have specific purposes in mind as well.

In addition to providing information for his readers, Nhuong's purpose is to keep his readers interested and entertained. In this nonfictional narrative, the events of Nhuong's life are written like a story, providing conflict, tension, and humor for his readers and thereby achieving his purpose of keep them interested and entertained.

EXERCISE 2

Read the following passage from the essay. Use what you have learned in this lesson to answer the questions that follow it.

When I had squeezed myself into the hole and had almost reached the cubs, the mother otter came up behind me and bit my toes, very hard! It was so painful that I had to crawl out of the hole as quickly as possible and shake her off. The mother otter jumped back into the river, but when I crawled into the hole again I received the same painful bite on my toes. Suddenly, I came up with an idea. I took some mud from the riverbank and wrote on Tank's back, *Otter cubs—come quickly*. Then I gave Tank a little tap on the back and said, "Go." Tank trotted straight home.

When Tank arrived home my parents saw the fish he carried, but no me. They panicked. Then they discovered the message on Tank's back, and they were very happy. My cousin and Tank soon returned to where I was. My cousin prevented the mother otter from biting me while I took the three cubs out of the hole, one by one.

1. Which of the five general purposes did the author have for writing this passage? Explain your answer.

2. What specific purpose do you think the author might have had for including this event in the story?

Now check your answers with your teacher. Review this lesson if you don't understand why an answer was incorrect.

WRITING ON YOUR OWN   2

In this exercise you will use what you have learned in this lesson to analyze the author's purposes for writing the selection you chose. Follow these steps:

- Analyze your selection to determine the author's general purpose for writing: to inform, instruct, entertain, express an opinion, or persuade.
- While determining the author's general purpose, also consider any specific purposes you think the author may have had in mind.
- Write a paragraph identifying the author's purposes. Give reasons to support your conclusions.

LESSON 3

AUTHOR'S THESIS

In Unit 4 you learned how the author organized the information in the article "Houston, We've Had a Problem" into main ideas with supporting details. You also learned that every nonfiction selection has a central idea that holds the piece together. Sometimes this central idea, or thesis, is directly stated, but often it is only implied. The author expects readers to be able to discover the thesis on their own.

When you are analyzing a piece of nonfiction, it is very important to identify the thesis. The thesis of "River Creatures" is not directly stated by Nhuong, but it is clearly implied. It might be stated this way: "The people of the village spent much of their time trying to get food, yet they never complained and seemed to enjoy working together and helping each other."

Good writers provide details that support their thesis. Do you think Nhuong provides enough details to support the thesis of "River Creatures"?

EXERCISE 3

Read this passage from the essay. Use what you have learned in this lesson to answer the questions that follow it.

In our hamlet, whenever an eel was hooked, the children of the neighborhood had a good time. They ran out of their houses when they heard the yell for help. Two or three boys would help pull out the eel, and everyone else yelled or laughed. Sometimes adults came to help too, if they were not busy. It took at least one hour to pull the eel out of its nest, and by this time, it was usually dead.

But a live eel got a better price than a dead one in the market, and since Tank had easily succeeded in pulling the white catfish out of the river for our old

friend, I came up with the idea of letting him drag eels
out of their nests for me. If he could pull an eel out
quickly, I had a better chance to get the eel alive
instead of dead.

1. How do the details of this passage support the thesis of
the essay as stated on page 213?

2. What details in these paragraphs tell you about the character of the author when he was a boy?

Now check your answers with your teacher. Review this
lesson if you don't understand why an answer was incorrect.

 WRITING ON YOUR OWN   3

In this exercise you will use what you have learned in this
lesson to analyze the thesis of the selection you chose.
Follow these steps:

• Analyze the selection to determine what its thesis is.
  Determine whether the author has provided enough
  details to support that thesis.
• Write one or two paragraphs identifying the thesis in the
  selection. State whether you think the author provided suf-
  ficient details to support the thesis. If you believe the
  author did, include some examples.

DISCUSSION GUIDES

- In a class discussion, talk about other fiction and nonfiction selections that you and others have read that also describe living in a foreign land. Compare and contrast that lifestyle with Nhuong's.
- In a small group discuss what it would be like to trade places with Nhuong. How well do you think each of you would adjust to your new lives? What do you think each of you would like most and least about your new lives? Explain your answers.
- The rather primitive, simple life described in this selection continues in some parts of the world. As a class discuss whether you think there will always be cultures that differ greatly from the modern world in their way of life. Do you think all cultures should adopt modern ways as soon as it is possible to do so? Explain your reasons.

WRITE AN ANALYSIS

In this exercise you will use what you have learned in this unit to write an analysis of a nonfictional selection and give a brief evaluation of it.

Follow these steps to complete your analysis. If you have any questions about the writing process, refer to Using the Writing Process on page 217.

- Gather and review the following pieces of writing you did in this unit: 1) the list of selection titles identified by type and kind of nonfiction, 2) the paragraphs describing the form of nonfiction used in your chosen selection, 3) the paragraph identifying the author's purposes, 4) the paragraphs identifying the thesis and any details in the selection.
- You have almost all you need to complete your analysis. Begin by writing a title: "An Analysis of (title of selection)."
- Write an opening paragraph in which you briefly summarize what the story is about and identify the form of nonfiction it is.
- Add the paragraph describing the author's purpose for writing.
- Add the paragraphs describing the thesis and any details. Include a few examples of those details.
- In your concluding paragraph write a brief evaluation of the selection. To *evaluate* is to judge the merit or worth of something. Simply give your opinion of the selection.
- Exchange your completed analysis with a classmate. Comment on each other's work and make suggestions for improvement. If any suggestions are good ones, revise your analysis accordingly.
- Proofread your final draft for errors in spelling, grammar, punctuation, and capitalization. Make a final copy and save it in your writing portfolio.

USING THE WRITING PROCESS

This reference section explains the major steps in the writing process. It will help you complete the writing exercises in this book. Read the information carefully so you can understand the process thoroughly. Whenever you need a quick review of important things to think about when you write, refer to the handy checklist on page 223.

Most tasks worth doing have several steps. For example, houses can be built only after the builder follows a number of complicated, logical steps. Moviemakers must go through a series of steps before releasing a film. Even a task as simple as making a peanut butter and jelly sandwich requires that the sandwich maker perform specific steps in order. So it should be no surprise that anyone who wants to write a good story, play, poem, report, or article must follow certain steps too. Taken together, the steps a writer follows are called the *writing process*. This writing process is divided into three main stages: prewriting, writing, and revising. Each stage is important for good writing.

STAGE 1: **Prewriting**

Prewriting consists of all the preparation you do before you put a single word down on paper. There are many decisions that you must make so that your writing is as interesting, logical, and easy to read as possible. Here are the steps you should take before you begin to write:

1. **Decide on your audience.** Who will read your writing? Will your audience be your teacher? Will it be readers of the school newspaper? Or will your audience be family or friends? Your writing will change, depending on who you think your audience will be.

2. **Decide on your purpose.** Why are you writing? Do you want to teach your audience something? Do you want to entertain

them? Do you want to change someone's mind about an issue? Think about your purpose before you begin to write.

3. **Think about possible topics.** What are some topics that interest you? Make a list of topics that you are familiar with and might like to write about. Make another list of topics that interest you and that you want to learn about.

   One technique that helps some writers at this stage is *brainstorming.* When you brainstorm, you let your mind wander freely. Without judging your ideas first, scribble them down as they come to you—even if they seem silly or farfetched. Good ideas often develop from unusual thoughts.

   If you're having trouble coming up with ideas by yourself, brainstorm with a partner or a group of classmates. Jot down everyone's ideas as they say them. Brainstorming alone or with others should give you a long list of possible writing topics.

4. **Choose and narrow your topic.** Once you have chosen a topic, you will probably find that it is impossible to cover every aspect of it in one piece of writing. Say, for example, you have chosen to write about the possibility of life on other planets. In a single piece, you could not possibly include everything that has been researched about extraterrestrial life. Therefore you must choose one or two aspects to focus on, such as alleged sightings in the United States or worldwide organizations that study extraterrestrial life. Otherwise you might overload your writing with too many ideas. Concentrate on telling about a few things thoroughly and well.

5. **Research your topic.** You probably have used an encyclopedia, the library, or the Internet to look up information for factual reports. But even when you write fictional stories, you often need to do some research. In a story set during the Civil War, for example, your characters wouldn't use

pocket cameras or wear suits of armor. In order to make your story as accurate and believable as possible, you would have to research how Americans lived and dressed during the years of the Civil War.

To conduct your research, you may want to use books, magazines, newspapers, reference works, or electronic sources. Some topics may require you to interview knowledgeable people. For realistic stories set in the present time, you may find that the best research is simple observation of everyday life. Thorough research will help ensure that your facts and details are accurate.

6. **Organize your research.** Once you have the facts, ideas, and details, you need to decide how to arrange them. Which order will you choose? No matter what you are writing, it is always helpful to begin with a written plan. If you are writing a story, you probably will tell it in time order. Make a list of the major story events, arranged from first to last.

Arranging details in time order is not the only way to organize information, however. Some writers start by making *lists* (informal outlines) of the facts and ideas they have gathered. Then they rearrange the items on their lists until they have an order that will work well in their writing.

Other writers make formal *outlines,* designating the most important ideas with roman numerals (I, II, III, IV, and so on) and related details with letters and numerals (A, B, C; 1, 2, 3; a, b, c; and so on). An outline is a more formal version of a list, and like the items in a list, the items in an outline can be rearranged until you decide on a logical order. Both outlines and lists help you organize and group your ideas.

Mapping or *clustering* is another helpful technique used by many writers. With this method, you write a main idea in the center of a cluster and then surround it with facts and ideas connected to that idea. Following is an example of a cluster map:

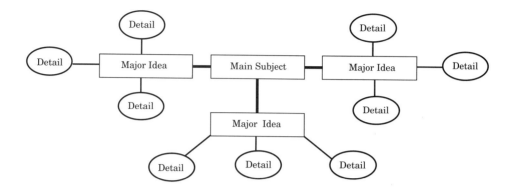

STAGE 2: Writing

1. **Get started.** Begin your writing with an introductory sentence or paragraph. A good introduction can become a guide for the rest of your piece. For ideas on good opening sentences, take a look at some of your favorite stories or magazine articles.

   Your introduction should give your audience a hint about what is coming next. If you are writing a story, your introduction should set the tone and mood. It should reveal the narrator's point of view, and it may introduce the main characters, the setting, and your purpose for writing. Do the best you can with your introduction, but remember that, if you wish to, you can always change it later.

2. **Keep writing.** Get your thoughts down as quickly as possible, referring to your prewriting notes to keep you on track. Later, when you are done with this *rough draft,* you will have a chance to revise and polish your work to make it as clear and accurate as possible. For right now, however, don't stop for spelling, grammar, or exact wording problems. Come as close as you can to what you want to say but don't let yourself get bogged down in details.

STAGE 3: Revising

Now you're ready to revise your work. Careful revision includes editing and reorganizing that can make a big difference in the final product. You may wish to get feedback from your classmates or your teacher about how to revise your work.

1. **Revise and edit your work.** When you are revising and editing, ask yourself these questions:
   - Did I follow my prewriting plan? Reread your entire first draft. Compare it to your original plan. Did you skip anything important? If you added an idea, did it work logically with the rest of your plan? Even if you decide that your prewriting plan is no longer what you want, it may include ideas you don't want to lose.
   - Is my writing clear and logical? Does one idea follow the other in a sensible order? Do you want to change the order or add ideas to make the organization clearer?
   - Is my language clear and interesting? Have you chosen exact verbs, nouns, and adjectives? For example, have you used forms of the verb *to be (is, are, being, become)* more often than you should? If so, replace them or change your sentence to make them unnecessary. Include precise action words such as *raced, hiked, zoomed,* and *hurried* in place of the overused verb *went.* Instead of using vague nouns such as *water* and *green,* choose exact ones such as *cascade* or *pond* and *lime.* Replace common adjectives such as *beautiful* and *nice* with precise ones such as *elegant, gorgeous,* and *lovely.*
   - Is my writing clear and to the point? Take out words that repeat the same ideas. For example, don't use both *liberty* and *freedom.* These words are synonyms. Choose one word or the other.

2. **Proofread for errors in spelling, grammar, capitalization, and punctuation.** Anyone reading your writing will notice such

errors immediately. These errors can confuse your readers or make them lose interest in what they are reading.

If you are in doubt about the spelling of a word, look it up or ask someone for help. If you are unsure about your grammar, read your writing aloud and listen carefully. Does anything sound wrong? Check with a friend or classmate if you need a second opinion—or refer to a grammar handbook.

Make sure every group of words is a complete sentence. Are any of your sentences run-ons? Do proper nouns begin with capital letters? Is the first word of every sentence capitalized? Do all your sentences have the correct end marks? Should you add any other punctuation to your writing to make your ideas even clearer? If your writing includes dialogue, have you used quotation marks correctly?

3. **Make a clean final draft to share.** After you are satisfied with your writing, it is time to share it with your audience. If you are lucky enough to be composing on a computer, you can print out a final copy easily, after running a spell-check. If you are writing your final draft by hand, make sure your handwriting is clear and easy to read. Leave margins on either side of the page. You may want to skip every other line. Make your writing look inviting to your readers. After all, you put a lot of work into this piece. It's important that people read and enjoy it.

A WRITING CHECKLIST

Ask yourself these questions before beginning a writing assignment:

- Have I chosen a topic that is both interesting and manageable? Should I narrow it so I can cover it in the space that I have?
- Do I have a clear prewriting plan?
- What should I do to gather my facts and ideas? By reading? interviewing? observing?
- How will I organize my ideas? In a list? an outline? a cluster map?
- Do I have an opening sentence or paragraph that will pull my readers in?
- Do I need to add more information? switch the order of paragraphs? take out unnecessary information?

Ask yourself these questions after completing a writing assignment:

- Did I use my prewriting plan?
- Is the organization of my writing clear? Should I move, add, or delete any paragraphs or sentences to make the ideas flow more logically?
- Do all the sentences in one paragraph relate to one idea?
- Have I used active, precise words? Is my language interesting? Do the words say what I mean?
- Are all the words spelled correctly?
- Have I used correct grammar, capitalization, punctuation, and formatting?
- Is my final draft legible, clean, and attractive?

GLOSSARY OF LITERARY TERMS

This glossary includes definitions for important literary terms that are introduced in this book. Boldfaced words within the definitions are other terms that appear in the glossary.

anecdote   a short account of some interesting incident or event. Like a short story, an anecdote has characters, a setting, and a plot. Writers use anecdotes to support their opinions and to add interest to their writing.

argument   the reasoning a writer uses to lead the reader to a logical conclusion.

article   a nonfiction work that informs or explains a subject to the reader. Articles are generally found in newspapers or magazines.

author's purpose   the writer's reason for creating a particular work. The purpose may be to inform, to entertain, to express an opinion, or to persuade readers to do or think something. An author may have more than one purpose for writing, but usually one is the most important.

autobiography   the story of a real person's life written by that person.

biography   the story of a real person's life written by someone else.

description   the kind of writing that helps readers picture a person, a place, or an event. The other basic kinds of writing are **narration, exposition,** and **argumentation.**

essay   a brief work of nonfiction that expresses a person's opinions or views about a particular subject. The purpose of an essay may be to analyze, to inform, to entertain, or to persuade.

evaluating   the process of judging the merit, or worth, of the facts and opinions that an author presents.

exaggeration   an intentional overstatement of facts or events so that their meanings are intensified.

example   events or instances that explain or specifically illustrate a general statement.

exposition   the kind of writing that presents information. The other basic kinds of writing are **narration, description,** and **argumentation.**

fact   a statement that can be proved.

figurative language   words or phrases used in unusual ways to create strong, vivid images. Figurative language focuses attention on certain ideas or compares things that are basically different.

foreshadowing   the use of hints or clues to suggest events that are going to happen later in the story. A writer uses foreshadowing to build suspense.

generalization   a broad statement or conclusion that is true of *some* or *most* but not *all* examples.

hyperbole   a figure of speech that deliberately exaggerates the truth in order to express an idea or feeling. "I've told you that a million times" is an example of hyperbole.

imagery   the use of words or phrases that appeal to one or more of a the senses of sight, hearing, taste, smell, and touch.

interpretation   one person's view of the meaning of certain words, events, or actions. Nonfiction writers continually interpret facts by explaining their meaning and evaluating their importance.

irony   the contrast between what appears to be and what really is or between what is expected and what actually happens. *See* **verbal irony** and **understatement.**

loaded language   the use of words and phrases that appeal to a reader's emotions.

metaphor   a comparison of two basically unlike things that does not use a word of comparison such as *like* or *as*. A metaphor suggests that one thing *is* another. The purpose of a metaphor is to suggest an unusual way of looking at one of the things.

narration   the kind of writing that gives the events and actions of a story. The other basic kinds of writing are **description, exposition,** and **argumentation.**

opinion   a statement about what someone thinks, but which cannot be proved or disproved.

personification   a figure of speech in which an animal, an object, or an idea is given the characteristics of a person. Personification can be used to add humor to a work or to describe abstract ideas.

persuasion   the kind of writing that tries to persuade readers to accept an author's opinion. Essayists, for example, often use persuasion to convince readers that their opinions are correct. The other basic kinds of writing are **narration, description,** and **exposition.**

primary source   information that comes directly from the time a subject lived or an event occured. *See* **secondary sources.**

profile   a brief account of a person's life. It focuses on the character of the subject and one or two major events rather than recalling all the details of that person's life.

secondary source   information that comes from a later time than a subject lived or an event occured. *See* **primary source.**

simile   a direct comparison between two unlike things that have some quality in common. Similes connect the two things by using the words *like*, *as*, or *than* or the verbs *appears* or *seems*. The purpose of a simile is to create a vivid new way of looking at one of the things.

subject   the person whose life story is being told in a **biography** or **autobiography.**

theme   the underlying message, or central idea, of a piece of writing.

thesis   the directly-stated purpose or main idea of an article or essay.

tone   the writer's attitude toward his or her subject or audience.

topic sentence   a sentence that states the main idea of a paragraph.

understatement   a type of **irony** in which something is represented as less than it really is.

verbal irony   a type of **irony** in which a writer or a character says one thing but means something entirely different.